CULTURE SHOCK!

New York
At your Door

Mark Cramer

Graphic Arts Center Publishing Company
Portland, Oregon

In the same series

Argentina	*Egypt*	*Laos*	*Sri Lanka*
Australia	*France*	*Malaysia*	*Sweden*
Bolivia	*Germany*	*Mauritius*	*Switzerland*
Borneo	*Greece*	*Mexico*	*Syria*
Britain	*Hong Kong*	*Morocco*	*Taiwan*
Burma	*India*	*Nepal*	*Thailand*
California	*Indonesia*	*Netherlands*	*Turkey*
Canada	*Iran*	*Norway*	*UAE*
Chile	*Ireland*	*Pakistan*	*Ukraine*
China	*Israel*	*Philippines*	*USA*
Cuba	*Italy*	*Singapore*	*USA—The South*
Czech Republic	*Japan*	*South Africa*	*Venezuela*
Denmark	*Korea*	*Spain*	*Vietnam*

Chicago At Your Door	*A Globe-Trotter's Guide*
Havana At Your Door	*A Parent's Guide*
Jakarta At Your Door	*A Student's Guide*
London At Your Door	*A Traveller's Medical Guide*
New York At Your Door	*A Wife's Guide*
Paris At Your Door	*Living and Working Abroad*
Rome At Your Door	*Working Holidays Abroad*

Illustrations by TRIGG
Cover photographs by HBL Network Photo Agency
Photographs by Mark Cramer

© 1999 Times Editions Pte Ltd
© 2000 Times Media Private Limited
Reprinted 2000

This book is published by special
arrangement with Times Media Private Limited
Times Centre, 1 New Industrial Road, Singapore 536196
International Standard Book Number 1-55868-502-2
Library of Congress Catalog Number 99-60173
Graphic Arts Center Publishing Company
P.O. Box 10306 • Portland, Oregon 97296-0306 • (503) 226-2402

Printed in Singapore

For my father, Syd Cramer,
who stood up to Robert Moses and won.

CONTENTS

ACKNOWLEDGMENTS

My thanks to the many people who helped me directly or indirectly with this project, some of whom include Ada, Art, Lee Habeeb, Margaret Shiba, the gracious New Yorkers who welcomed my prying camera, a guard at Shea Stadium, a swimming pool attendant in Queens, the owner of a photo developing store in the East Village, a woman walking her dog in the upper west section of Central Park, a bus driver in Queens, the attendants at a Dominican *botanica* in Washington Heights, a Bronx city planner, two women at a Greenwich Village restaurant, a hip priest in Hoboken, a former jazz club owner, the reference librarians in Bethlehem, New York, editor Ken Chang, who helped make this project challenging and enjoyable, and my lifetime partner Martha Sonia, my faithful critic.

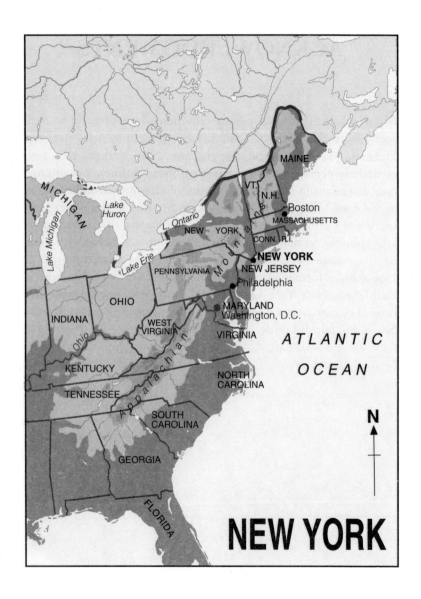

INTRODUCTION

A decade ago at a get-together in my Los Angeles home, it suddenly occurred to me that most of my friends were ex-New Yorkers. I prided myself on being universal, and shuddered at the thought that the way I chose my friends, and by extension, the way I led my life, had much more to do with the city of my upbringing than my personal choice.

Some of us were Jewish, others Irish, others Italian, and yet others Puerto Rican. Yet we shared some mysterious commonality that transcended ethnic background.

Some years later, I visited my chess master friend Edgard in the Detroit suburb of Livonia, Michigan. Edgard felt out of place in his new neighborhood. He missed New York. Never mind that he was from Colombia, South America. Mired in a region without public transportation, Edgard longed for the luxury of hopping onto a subway and gliding and thumping to his destination. For several years he had fought against using his car to go for groceries or to pick up a newspaper, something he could do in Manhattan by strolling to the corner on streets that were an extension of his apartment. In sprawling Livonia, many of whose streets don't even have sidewalks, he finally succumbed and began to drive.

I thought back to Southern California, where most of those who used public transportation were bums, Salvadoran cleaning ladies, or ex-New Yorkers like me. Could it be that my preference for public transportation was New York-determined and had nothing to do with my individuality? While 53 percent of New Yorkers use public transportation, only 34 percent use it in Boston, where they have a superb subway system. And in Edgard's Detroit, only 12 percent of the population uses public transportation.

In Southern California I had gotten to know two "friendly neighborhood bookies" and coincidentally, I thought, both were New Yorkers by upbringing, just like the character played by Woody Allen in *The Front*. I had thought that my identity as a studious gambler was an individual choice, not a function of my New York background.

The bookie coincidence obligated me to consider my youth in New York. It was only natural for us to bet on any and everything, from basketball to horse racing. We played three-card monte on buses and we gambled with baseball cards. Some of the cards I lost would be worth a fortune today. I recalled scenes from James Caan's classic movie *The Gambler*, and wouldn't you know it, the film took place in New York.

But the ease with which I used public transportation or wagered on a horse race were innocuous facets of my culture or subculture. Could other more behavioral idiosyncrasies be attributed to my New York upbringing rather than to my individuality?

There was the time as a Spanish professor at a faculty meeting in California that I volunteered an idea that seemed very obvious to me.

"Our language method is not working," I said. "Most of our students feel disabled by a method based on pure pattern memorization with no understanding as to the *why*."

I expected an "amen" from the rest of the faculty members. But my pronouncement was met with cold, daggerlike silence. The teaching method I was criticizing happened to be the invention of our chairman, Dr. D., who was present at the meeting. To criticize a scholar's teaching method is like telling a mother her baby is ugly.

Recalling the incident, I am forced to consider that mine was the behavior of a typical uncouth New Yorker. When the academic year had ended and the damage was done, my colleagues got together (without me) and staged a faculty coup d'etat, removing Dr. D. from the position of chair. Their first order of business was to dump his teaching method.

Had I been heard at the original meeting, they could have changed the method without deposing Dr. D. (whom I thought was a good man). That's the way we would have done it in New York.

My uncouth, misanthropic behavior at the faculty meeting might be vindicated by the former Californian transplanted to New York, editor Ian Blair, who explains:

"In California people say 'Hava a nice day' and they really mean 'Fuck you.' But in New York they say 'Fuck you' and they really mean 'Have a nice day.'"

Could this be why New Yorkers can't get elected president or vice-president? Think of Al Smith, Thomas Dewey, Geraldine Ferraro, or Nelson Rockefeller. The rest of the nation seems to hold a grudge against New Yorkers. The eloquent but outspoken Mario Cuomo made a smart move by not running for the big prize even though his dedicated admirers urged him to do so.

Of course, resentment against New Yorkers may run deeper than a proper southern aversion to the uncouth. New York is considered by some non-New Yorkers as an imperial power within the nation. If New Yorkers hold so much financial, artistic, and media power, they cannot be permitted to monopolize politics as well.

This is not my idea. I have been with people at cocktail parties who were unaware of my New York heritage. With a remarkable lack of inhibitions, they said all kinds of nasty things about New York, from behavioral to ethnic slurs.

During the past decade, I have been travelling back to New York and remaining there for lengthier periods each time. This book represents a mission of rediscovery, an attempt to decipher the enigma of the place that has evidently had so much influence on the way I behave and make decisions. My goal is to provide substantial practical insights, along with a less tangible awareness that will aid the newcomer in adjusting to this thrilling city. I feel I've got a double advantage in this enterprise, having grown up here but also having had to readjust to New York after having resided in foreign places like South America, Europe and, yes, California. You'll find a profusion of pragmatic advice and objective information here; but if I seem opinionated at times, I must be pardoned, for after all, I am a New Yorker.

Chapter One

IN SEARCH OF NEW YORK:

Sense of Place and State of Mind

I'm moving out of New York to Wisconsin, where I can live among real Americans.

— New York man at a Queens swimming pool

New York is a city of distinct neighborhoods. Typical introductions to New York correctly begin with a description of key neighborhoods. Thematically, I shall not diverge, but my presentation of New York neighborhoods focuses on economic and cultural turf wars that seem to dominate the history of most neighborhoods. Either citizens are struggling to make important changes in their community, or they are entrenched in a battle to prevent such changes.

Newcomers to New York will unwittingly become involved in these sometimes subtle, other times open, turf wars. Just by choosing a neighborhood, you may become an agent of gentrification in a community that favors or opposes such a change. Or you may be the agent of ethnic transformation that will either cause social friction or stimulate a dynamic cultural awakening.

Before we visit some of the New York neighborhoods you may choose to visit or reside in, we shall have a glimpse at the overall physical setting of this city and its metropolitan area, from the perspective of a series of anomalies that raise the issue of whether New York is a physical place, a state of mind, or both.

Any encyclopedia will tell you that multicultural New York is composed of five boroughs, four of them located on islands, with only the Bronx on the mainland of New York State. You'll be told that the total population of the five boroughs stands at about 8 million, with that figure rising to 20 million when the whole New York Metropolitan Area is considered.

ANOMALIES

1. Why is New York City, the financial and arts capital of the world, not even the capital of the state which bears its name? That official function is left to Albany, a much smaller city about 130 miles (209 kilometers) north of Manhattan up the Hudson River.
2. Why do New York's two professional football teams (the New York Giants and the New York Jets), play their *home* games at the Meadowlands, which is actually across the river in another state (New Jersey)?
3. Why do people from Brooklyn and Queens, on their way to Manhattan, say "we're going to the city" if Brooklyn and Queens are boroughs belonging to the city?
4. Why do people from Brooklyn and Queens, on their way to the beaches of Nassau or Suffolk Counties, say "we're going

to Long Island" (a.k.a. "the Island"), if both Brooklyn and Queens are part of Long Island?

5. What is the strange relationship between New York City and its suburbs (Nassau and Suffolk Counties on Long Island, Westchester County in mainland New York State, Fairfield County in Connecticut, and Hudson, Essex, and Union Counties in New Jersey)? Are these places mere satellites of the city or distinct communities?

6. Why have so many New Yorkers never visited Staten Island (Richmond County)? And why is there a movement among residents of Staten Island to secede from the city?

7. If we do not consider six U.S. counties whose heritage was Hispanic long before any Anglo settlements, the Bronx, with 570,000 Hispanics, has the second largest Hispanic population of any U.S. county. (Number one on the list is Cook County, which includes the whole city of Chicago.) Lacking in original Hispanic heritage and not contiguous to any Latin country, how has New York drawn so many immigrants from Latin America?

Not So Simple Questions . . .

Most of these questions have no simple answers, and merely point to the fact that New York's physical and human geography are as much a state of mind as they are a place with fixed boundaries. More realistic from a standpoint of defined city boundaries are New York's neighborhoods, which are the most fundamental and dynamic units within the larger city.

A VISIT TO SOME NEIGHBORHOODS

Growing up in New York, I learned the concept of turf. The kids in my neighborhood were white, and the ones a few blocks down, on other streets not much different than ours, were also white. But those kids never came around to our turf, and we never crossed the invisible border to theirs. We had no idea at the time what caused such division. We were middle class, and they were a few notches above us, with larger yards and houses of more character, but we never considered such nuances would make a difference. Our neighborhood was of mixed religions, with Catholics, secular Jews, and Protestants; theirs was virtually 100 percent Catholic. But none of us were ever conscious of any religious barriers.

For whatever cause, we received pencil-scribbled notes from the kids who lived a few blocks away. They were coming into our neighborhood to teach us a lesson. We all met to plan our strategy. None of us had knives. One of the kids, Warren, who wanted to be part of our group, had a handgun. He was a friend of mine but I was made to understand that he was not our type, and my friendship with him remained one-to-one only. (I remember our sixth grade teacher warning the class—with my friend Warren present—that Warren was going to become a "juvenile delinquent" and that we should be careful of whom we chose as friends.)

In preparation for the attack, we built makeshift weapons like slingshots, and we set up piles of stones in safe places behind bushes. The hour of attack arrived and we waited. After a few hours we realized that they were never going to carry out their threat. We assumed at the time that we had won a moral victory. But they too assumed the same thing, and they might have been right, for as a group, we never strayed onto their turf.

Today, New Yorkers wishing a reprieve from such neighborhood tribalism without having to move to a multicultural community come to Skate Circle in Central Park, where all ages (teenagers and old hippies), all social classes (stockbrokers and street vendors), all races and ethnic groups, and even a few Fifth Avenue celebrities, skate around in concentric circles. Writer John Tierney calls this a metaphor for New York's "parallel lives" and reminds the observer who may be too prone to idealism that most of these roller skaters, who dance together to boom box music just south of the 72nd Street transverse and west of the bandshell, will return to their more monocultural "statuspheres" after their brief bouts with the global family.

Back in their chosen neighborhoods they will once again confront any of the various types of turf confrontations that typify some of New York's more interesting neighborhoods.

SoHo

SoHo, in Lower Manhattan, represents the prototypical evolution of many New York neighborhoods. The streets were in disrepair and buildings were on the demolition list. Rents were low. So artists in need of cheap lofts moved in, and refurbished old factories and crumbling tenements. They opened funky cafes and the street scene became colorful and animated.

The same commercial interests that had previously shunned the neighborhood now move in. They establish more mainstream businesses, buy and renovate cheap buildings, and within a year or two the rents have skyrocketed. Many of the original pioneers of the neighborhood, the artists and those who simply wish to live an artistic, non-materialistic life, are obligated to move out when confronted with the new rent paradigm.

I visited SoHo at the tail end of its bohemian period, looking for a vestige of counterculture New York. What I found was a place so manicured that even fruit stands and bakeries were zoned to look like art galleries. I wanted to sit at a typical SoHo cafe and sip a straight espresso. But all the outdoor cafe tables were occupied by sleek men and women dressed in black. The starving artists had long since fled to the East Village.

Two signs illustrated the change in the neighborhood. In one gallery was a poster: "MONEY CREATES TASTE" and on a nearby wall, graffiti announced "KILL ALL ARTISTS."

SoHo stands for "South of Houston" Street and is located south of Houston and north of the flea market Canal Street, at the same longitude as Washington Square—in other words, in the outhernmost part of Greenwich Village. Contemporary art museums, including a branch of the Guggenheim, have moved to SoHo, and the neighborhood is still worth visiting.

But high-end stores like Louis Vuitton, Yves Saint Laurent, Prada, Helena Rubenstein and the jewelers H. Stern and Bulgari are also moving in.

"Around SoHo these days," wrote Terry Pristin, "a good number of old-timers are more than a little upset that all of this is happening to a place that has long defined itself as an antidote to uptown taste in art and fashion."

As can be expected in New York's turf warfare, an organization called the SoHo Alliance is digging trenches in an attempt to protect the neighborhood's funky character, with members openly proclaiming that they do not want to live in a chic neighborhood like the Upper East Side.

But the war seems lost. Huge billboards are today invading the neighborhood, with sleek fashion ads that remind onlookers of the pages of *Elle* magazine. "They're making this space into Times Square," complained artist and businessman Marc Balet, and community complaints about SoHo's corporatization keep flowing into City Hall.

East Village

By now, most of SoHo's funky pioneers have fled north and east to what they labeled the East Village, resolved to prevent a reenactment of SoHo in their new adopted community. They arrived to a place that was besieged by drug pushers, alcoholics, and crumbling tenements. They have become but one of the groups that has participated in the rapid evolution of this neighborhood, as documented by its various conflicting names.

This community, centered around Tomkins Square, was once considered the northern part of the proletarian-immigrant neighborhood called the Lower East Side. With north-south avenues labeled by letters from A through D, locals rebaptized the neighborhood Alphabet City. And with a recent influx of Dominican immigrants, yet another parallel name was ascribed to the community: Loisaida, a Spanish transliteration for Lower East Side.

For two decades now, various sectors of the East Village population have been positioning themselves in the struggle to define the neighborhood. Established immigrants and new immigrants, hippies and yuppies, drug dealers and police, quirky artists and slick developers, squatters and housing activists are pitted in a multifaceted struggle, whose central battle ground is Tomkins Square.

On a recent visit to Tomkins Square I saw local old-timers playing chess, salsa musicians working on a new arrangement, grizzly alcoholics with disheveled beards, and a prim young couple walking a well-groomed husky. Fate had dealt a better hand to the pampered canine than the bearded homeless men who watched him prance by. On nearby streets, empty lots had been occupied by community gardens, some of which had won prizes in local contests. Dominican youths hung out on the street while their elders chatted on brownstone stoops.

Dominican youths adopt the New York custom of using the street as a public hangout

"The persistence of a multicutural proletarian quarter near the current government and financial core of the country's largest metropolitan center is a stunning anomaly," wrote Janet L. Abu-Lughod in *From Urban Village to East Village: the Battle for New York's Lower East Side* (1994).

Gentrification is encroaching the East Village from the west, with St. Marks Place looking like a corporate shopping mall, sporting its tee-shirt stores and clothing chains. But older Eastern European immigrants, newer Puerto Rican and Dominican residents, and artist refugees from SoHo share a commitment with community activists to prevent the gentrification of their old buildings.

SoHo and the East Village are two neighborhoods highlighted in Cy Yoakam's **Lower Manhattan City Culture Map** (see pages 22–23). Yoakam publishes the journal *Urban Quality Indicators*, an indispensable source for anyone who uses quality of life as a criterion for deciding where to live or visit. Yoakam is a professor at the University of Michigan, and many of the foremost experts on urban quality of life are contributors to his fine publication. A yearly subscription to *Urban Quality Indicators* costs $29. Write to: 1756 Plymouth Road, #239, Ann Arbor, MI 48105 (or inquire at CYoakam578@aol.com). Individual back issues may also be ordered, depending on the cities and themes of interest to the reader. As can be seen in Yoakam's map, the concept of parallel lives is alive and well in compact Lower Manhattan, with so many distinct ethnic and social groups within such a reduced area.

Upper East Side

The Upper East Side is what community activists from SoHo and the East Village are trying not to become. I've got colleagues and cousins on the Upper East Side who would disagree with the bad rap their neighborhood gets from other New Yorkers.

"I've thought about this a lot," wrote Richard Laermer in his *Native's Guide to New York: Advice with attitude for people who live here — and visitors alike.* "People who live on the Upper East Side hate crowds . . . and won't even travel below 14th Street [the East Village and SoHo, for example] or above 95th Street (wrong side of the tracks, dear)."

The affluent core of the Upper East Side extends from 60th to 86th Street between Fifth Avenue and Lexington, and encompasses some of New York's best boutiques, galleries, and museums (the Guggenheim, the Whitney, and the Metropolitan are but a few).

"If we lived in this neighborhood," asked my son as we walked to the Whitney Museum, "we'd be considered poor, wouldn't we?"

Inside the Whitney Museum of American Art, we saw a number of paintings and photographs with more proletarian identities than the neighborhood outside — notably the fine permanent collection of works of Edward Hopper.

I still believe the Upper East Side gets a bad rap. No one made me feel unwanted in the great produce stores and bakeries along Lexington Avenue. But some of the neighborhood's own residents are partly to blame for the Upper East Side's uppity reputation. On April 4, 1998, Elaine Kaufman, the 69-year-old owner of Elaine's ("a watering hole for the literati and glitterati"), slapped a Mr. Jim Sorrels after a dispute at the bar just after midnight. Mr. Sorrels, 49, emerged from the argument with three long scratches on his right cheek. The argument evidently began when Mr. Sorrels's date didn't want a drink because she was driving that night. According to witnesses, Mrs. Kaufman called them "white trash." The maitre d'hotel at Elaine's defended his boss, telling police that he heard Sorrels "yelling at her."

South Bronx

The South Bronx is only six subway stops and within walking distance from the Upper East Side, but what a world of difference! During the 1980s, the South Bronx was considered one of

21

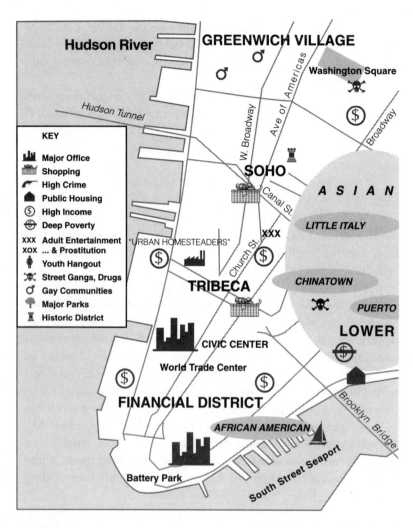

KEY

🏢	Major Office
🏛	Shopping
🔫	High Crime
🏠	Public Housing
$	High Income
⊕	Deep Poverty
XXX XOX	Adult Entertainment ... & Prostitution
🧍	Youth Hangout
☠	Street Gangs, Drugs
♂	Gay Communities
🌲	Major Parks
♜	Historic District

Hangouts. Some areas of Lower Manhattan, such as South Street Seaport, SoHo, Chinatown, and Greenwich Village (one of the most famous gay neighborhoods in the U.S.), might be considered national hangouts. The Lower Eastside (at 2nd and Houston) is also a hangout for some of Manhattan's "lower-class" prostitutes. (The "upper-class" ones are 2-3 miles up on 2nd Ave.) The city's homeless are concentrated in the East Village and the Lower Eastside.

Compiled by Cy Yoakam. Sources: U.S. Census, New York Times, New York City: Street Smarts, Guide to American Bordellos, Comparative Metropolitan Atlas, The American Street Gang, and base map from Maplitude of Caliper Corp.

Lower Manhattan City Culture Map

© 1997 by Urban Quality Indicators

Crime. Chinatown is home to five or six Chinese street gangs. Sociologist Malcolm Klein has found these gangs to be very territorial, with each controlling about six to ten Chinatown blocks. Drug dealing occurs in many places in East Village, the lower Eastside, and in and around Washington Park. As for white-collar crime, try Wall Street.

Ethnic Groups. Lower Manhattan has seen many ethnic neighborhoods come and go. Only traces of some groups remain (e.g., Eastern Europeaners); others hang on doggedly despite shrinkage (e.g., Little Italy and the Jewish residences/shops on Orchard Street). An expanding neighborhood is Chinatown, with 100,000 (mostly Chinese) residents, spilling north into Little Italy and east into the Lower Eastside, also home to many Puerto Ricans and other Hispanics.

23

the most dangerous neighborhoods in the world, as illustrated in films like *Fort Apache, The Bronx*. George Steinbrenner, owner of the New York Yankees, periodically threatens to pull his team out of historic Yankee Stadium because fans allegedly fear coming to the neighborhood. Tom Wolfe's novel *The Bonfire of the Vanities* painted the neighborhood as an urban jungle.

During that period, I was given a drive-through by a former college roommate, who had become a South Bronx property owner. Alleys with drug deals going down, empty lots with broken beer bottles, boarded-up buildings, and surly-looking youth hanging out on street corners — mainly Latinos and blacks — were some of the images I remember. I wondered whether my friend was part of the solution or part of the problem, as he collected rents from substandard housing while describing the neighborhood with raw cynicism.

I returned to the South Bronx in 1995 and again in 1998. What I saw corroborated what visionary city planner Bernd Zimmerman had told me in an interview — that the Bronx's renovation projects are intended "to get rid of the psychological, social and physical barriers" that have plagued urban renewal plans of the past.

The first visible evidence of the rebirth of the South Bronx was Hostos Community College. Unlike social-fortress-like culture centers, Hostos was intended as a cultural anchor for strong interactions between community artists and business people, blending culture and community activism.

The Grand Concourse, once a magnificent Champs Elysees-style boulevard with magnificent art deco architecture, had been blighted in the '70s, but today was no longer a dangerous place for a stroll. Boarded-up buildings were gone. Seven areas within the South Bronx were designated historic districts. Two of these areas have a healthy ethnic mix, in a community that is overall 44 percent Latino and 37 percent African-American.

Falling crime figures bode well for the South Bronx, but it is still perceived as a perilous neighborhood, and Yankee owner George Steinbrenner continues to use such fears in his attempts to extort city financing for a new stadium.

Long Island

Hundreds of thousands of New Yorkers wishing to escape the city's congestion and crime eventually found a new home on Long Island (with some of the earliest of these refugees coming from the South Bronx).

Levittown, Long Island was the site of the most notable of the early U.S. suburban experiments. Herbert Gans's study of the first three thousand families to move to Levittown illustrated that while such communities were well-conceived for young adults and small children, they became "Endsville" for youths who had "No place to go, nothing to do." In typical suburbs, parents acquired a new job title: chauffeur. Neither children nor teenagers could walk to the corner grocery store or newsstand as business was zoned out of residential streets. Curved streets doubled walking time to commercial avenues. Recreational facilities were often beyond walking distance; with no public transportation, parents were obligated to use their cars for each and every need of their children, and for even the simplest of their own needs as well.

After I had left home for college, my parents moved to Long Island. Without conceptualizing the sociological consequences of suburbia, I feared that my youngest brother would have nothing to do and would need his mother as a chauffeur for his basic needs. So I'd take my brother places in the city during my occasional visits. On one visit, I got tickets for a symphony orchestra concert at Carnegie Hall in Manhattan. I drove my brother to Queens, and we boarded the subway to "New York." To my surprise, my suburban brother became frightened by the rumbling noise of the trains and the menacing crowds.

It was then that I realized that my brother's upbringing was diametrically opposed to my own. To his credit, as a young adult, he worked as a courier in Manhattan, where he used the subways to deliver packages. But to this day he avoids the city when he can, and resides in suburban Westchester County.

The flat south side of Long Island is attractive for its Atlantic Ocean beaches, while the more affluent north side is graced with cliffs overlooking the Long Island Sound and hilly terrain. The north side is more woodsy thanks to its large estates.

Long Island is perceived to be a safe place, but it is not free of blighted pockets. In all my years of growing up in the city and looking for trouble, I was never the victim of a robbery. But my Long Island brother was held up once by violent attackers when working at a convenience store.

Aside from these anecdotal exceptions, Long Island, comprised of Nassau and Suffolk Counties, may be the most wealthy piece of real estate in the world. Long Island alone contains six of the richest 25 towns in the United States. No other suburb of New York City, not even Westchester County, has any towns that make this list. (Of the wealthiest 50 towns in the United States, 12 are found in Long Island—a whopping 24 percent.)

The six Long Island towns breaking into the top 25 are Matinecock, North Hills, Old Brookville, Old Westbury, Brookville, and Upper Brookville. Matinecock's median home price is $1,070,000 while less-wealthy Upper Brookville's median home value is $765,000. Secluded estates along winding, tree-lined country roads are worth considerably more than the median. Many residents of the Upper East Side in Manhattan have summer homes on Long Island. If one were to search for the power elite of New York City, the search would surely begin on the north shore of Long Island.

125th Street, Harlem

Every country and city in the world is a "land of contrasts" and it is virtually impossible to find a travel guide or article that does not use this stale cliche. But I cannot imagine a greater contrast than between the north shore hills of Long Island and 125th Street in Harlem.

Once the center of the Harlem Renaissance and still the home of the venerable Apollo Theater, 125th Street has long been one of the most troublesome and blighted areas of New York.

Today's 125th Street faces a typical Third World dilemma during a period of neoliberal economics. The 125th Street Business Improvement District is attempting to revitalize the neighborhood through loans and technical support to business people. But with the presence of this "empowerment zone," rents have gone up and local businesses are finding it difficult to compete with corporate outsiders.

This is the classic situation in which a Third World country opens its borders to foreign competition, and the foreigners arrive with greater financial leverage than the locals. The situation worsened for smaller local businesses when street vendors were removed by the city in 1995 to a special 116th Street market. With the loss of the street vendors, fewer pedestrians strolled by, and the sales volume of local businesses declined.

"We created the market," said one local business owner, "and now other people are coming in to reap the benefits."

One local entrepreneur, Dorothy Pittman Hughes had to mortgage her house to save her 16-year-old business, Harlem Office Supply. Anticipating the arrival of office supply chain stores whose national advertising campaigns cost little to local franchises and whose high-volume purchases allow for lower prices, Ms. Pittman Hughes adopted a revolutionary strategy fitting of her renaissance mentality.

The historic Apollo Theater, where many great African-American performers got their start.

She took her store public and sold shares on the premises of her business, at $1 apiece, with the ultimate goal that the community would own 29 percent of her business. Shareholders will naturally think twice before patronizing a rival business run by outsiders.

Furthermore, Ms. Pittman Hughes hopes that when stores like The Gap and Blockbuster arrive on 125th Street, neighbors will demand their share in these business before they start patronizing. Schools have taken entire classes to Harlem Office Supply, with each student purchasing his or her dollar share in what figures to be a revolutionary experiment in grass roots community business.

Washington Heights

Until Washington Heights becomes an empowerment zone, street vendors will not be removed from this exciting neighborhood with a mainly Dominican component. Up North Broadway, the street economy is alive and well.

Washington Heights extends from 155th Street to the upper tip of Manhattan, along the Hudson River. Hikers beginning The Long Path at the Washington Bridge can fill their backpacks with goods from any of the ma-and-pa groceries in this community. Rental agencies can find you rooms by the week or month for as little as $65 per week (average $100). Colorful *botánicas* sell religious art and medicinal herbs. Long distance phone shops abound, hawking cut-rate international calls. Stairways lead up a hill around 190th Street, where the Cloisters medieval museum nestles in Fort Tryon Park.

Drug pushers were a problem in several poorer sections of the neighborhood in the mid-1990s, but the fame of Dominican home run slugger Sammy Sosa brought attention to the plight of the neighborhood and help may be on the way.

Long Island City-Astoria

Will Long Island City be the next hot spot? Once a tough neighborhood with gang problems, artists moved in for their typical rescue. At the edge of Long Island City, overlooking the East River and the Manhattan skyline beyond, an illegal dumping ground blighted the neighborhood. Sculptor Marc di Suvero organized residents to get rid of the dump. Hundreds of volunteers from nearby neighborhoods worked for a year with a brigade of artists, picking up debris, planting grass and trees, and painting rocks.

The result was Socrates Sculpture Park, listed as one of the best public places in the U.S. by author Gianni Longo in *A Guide to Great American Public Places*. The success of contiguous Astoria could spill over into Long Island City. Astoria, a primarily Greek community, is benefiting from the rediscovery of important landmarks: the Steinway mansion and piano factory and the reacti-

Socrates Sculpture Park, a former city dump converted into an entertaining park by community activists.

vated Kaufman-Astoria TV and Movie Studios. Astoria cafes and restaurants are also spicing up this blue-collar neighborhood which is reached by the N line elevated train. I counted more than 20 different types of ethnic restaurants, including Mexican, Lebanese, Indian, and of course, Greek.

The Isamu Noguchi Garden Museum, near the Socrates Park, is another sculpture garden that could draw artists to the neighborhood. The formula that might get Long Island City past the revitalization barrier would include old factories converted into lofts and apartments plus one more art museum that decides to move to this old factory community. Wagers are being taken on the future of Long Island City.

Rockaway Beach

Turf wars have been the metaphor of this visit to New York neighborhoods. A variation on the theme is the surf war. The "Rockapulco" surfers are youths predominantly of Irish working-class background. In California, one finds another beach and avoids a surf war. But Rockaway Beach in Queens is one of New York's only decent surfing spots; only several of the beaches along the seven mile stretch are worthy of this displaced California sport, especially between Beaches 89 and 92. Californians will find it hard to believe that Duke Ellington's "Take the A Train" would turn out to be the instruction for arriving at the Rockaway Beach surfers' haven.

Outsiders who come to Rockaway Beach to test the waves are labeled "Brooklyn surfers," whether they are Italians or Jews from Brooklyn, Haitian or Jamaican "wave snakers" from the Bronx, or Manhattanite yuppies.

Clashes between the locals and the "Brooklyn surfers" have nothing to do with ethnicity and everything to do with controlling the space to catch a good wave. Rockaway is an isthmus jutting southwest from JFK Airport where one's turf is the surf.

31

ETHNIC NEIGHBORHOODS

Arthur Avenue

Arthur Avenue is New York's most authentic Italian neighborhood, located just west of the Bronx Zoo. Outsiders come here to shop with personal attention from Italian greengrocers, butchers, fish mongers, and bakers. The food at attractive Arthur Avenue restaurants is as good or better than more upscale counterparts in Manhattan, and the old neighborhood atmosphere is real.

Brighton Beach

Brighton Beach is a Russian and Jewish neighborhood with famous outdoor produce markets, thrift stores, rows of six-story apartment buildings, and old-timers playing cards on the beach. It's a long subway ride from Manhattan, but the beach is worth it. A short walk along the surf takes you to Coney Island, with its historic, funky amusement park, animated boardwalk, and of course, the beach.

Boro Park

Boro Park in Brooklyn is the home of the United States' largest community of Hasidic and non-Hasidic Orthodox Jews. For many of New York's secular Jews, Boro Park's Orthodox community represents an exotic and foreign culture. Shopping at a kosher butcher shop is one of New York's great ethnic experiences.

Chinatown

Chinatown in Lower Manhattan is considered by writer Henry Han Xi Lau as a ghetto. "I am ghetto" he writes, even though he has assimilated into university life. Han Xi Lau writes that most Chinatown kids fall into four categories: nerds who study to get into Ivy League schools, recent immigrants with their uncombed hair and crooked teeth, punks with their odd hair styles, and gangsters whom everyone tries to avoid. Han Xi Lau's karate friends return to the hood with their hair in punk style asymmetrical cuts and long, random strands. Together they engage in "grilling," or the "fine art of staring others down." As students they fit into the nerd category, but they identify with the punks.

Other New Yorkers go to Chinatown for its festivals and shops, or to eat. One of the best strategies to assure an authentic Chinese dining experience is to go where the menu is in Chinese only. Whatever you get will be what native Chinese folks like to eat.

El Barrio
Also known as "Spanish Harlem," El Barrio is a primarily Puerto Rican neighborhood of tenements and housing projects. El Barrio's busiest street is 116th Street, where you can shop for Caribbean specialties at La Marqueta. The Museo del Barrio is at Fifth Avenue and 104th Street. Check bulletin boards in grocery stores for the best spots to dance salsa. Puerto Ricans are the most disenfranchised ethnic group in the city and parts of El Barrio are not known for their public safety. The election of the visionary Nydia Velazquez to Congress in 1992 might be a prelude to the enfranchisement of the Puerto Rican community.

Other Ethnic Communities
With more than 100 ethnic groups in New York, a full menu of the city's ethnic neighborhoods is not possible. A few other notable communities are Koreatown on West 32nd Street in Manhattan, a Black-Caribbean neighborhood in the Bedford-Stuyvesant area of Brooklyn, and an Arab enclave on Atlantic Avenue in Brooklyn.

MULTICULTURAL NEIGHBORHOODS
Beyond the choice of a specific neighborhood is a broader decision. Would you prefer to live in a neighborhood dominated by a

single ethnic group, or one that is multicultural? Both options have their pluses and are available in New York. If you are a crosscultural person and enjoy fitting in with a traditional way of life, the menu of ethnic neighborhoods is comprehensive.

On the other hand, multicultural communities may offer more variety, while allowing the individual more diverse lifestyle options. A few of New York's multicultural neighborhoods are profiled here.

Greenwich Village

People complain that the rents in Greenwich Village, the area to the east, west, and south of Washington Square, are too high. But ever since beat writers like Jack Kerouac and jazz musicians like Thelonius Monk made the neighborhood an alternative tourist attraction, apartments have been at a premium. Yes, there are dog obedience classes for the yuppies in Washington Square, but grungy chess players and rambling musicians are also regulars in the park. Gentrified or no, Greenwich village remains a dynamic, artsy, multiethnic neighborhood with some semblance of a counterculture ambience. A cadre of Village old-timers entrenched in their anarchist ways and an annual replenishment of youth (thanks to the presence New York University) keep the streets lively. The Blue Note replaces the Village Gate and the Five Spot as the world's premier jazz club, and night life thrives throughout the Village. Despite the tourist traps, Greenwich Village is still a great place, especially after sundown. Its asymmetrical streets, laid out along the lines of 18th century farm paths, keep the neighborhood full of surprise turns and quirky nooks and crannies.

During the 1960s, gays added another significant cultural dimension to the neighborhood, but in recent years a large part of the Village's gay population has moved north to the more predictable Chelsea district.

Park Slope

Park Slope is a typical brownstone neighborhood in Brooklyn with an atypical mix of races, ethnic groups and social classes. This area contains the other immense New York park designed by Frederick Law Olmsted and Calvert Vaux: Prospect Park. Culture lovers can find plenty to do in this community without the necessity of crossing the East River to Manhattan. The Brooklyn Botanical Garden, the Brooklyn Museum, the Central Library, and major bookstores are all within the confines of this neighborhood, as are continuing education opportunities (see Interactive Directory).

Housing options go from the more expensive in the northern part of Park Slope to more moderate in the southern sector, with improving neighborhoods immediately south of Park Slope offering the best bargains.

Upper West Side

Manhattan's Upper West Side is the traditional turf of New York's ultraliberals, who have been under siege ever since the 1980s, when the "L" word became unpopular. This neighborhood extends roughly from 72nd Street to 110th Street, with the elegant Central Park West as the easternmost north-south avenue and the Hudson River to the west.

I stayed in this neighborhood for research purposes and found it rewarding on several accounts. Smaller and inexpensive theaters on North Broadway offered interesting new plays by local authors. The former Audobon Ballroom, scene of the 1965 murder of Malcolm X, has been converted into an eclectic nightclub, with jazz, salsa, and karaoke, depending on the evening you attend. Within a few blocks, I found a building inhabited by Mexican laborers, a wild religious service of Hasidic Jews, a modest meeting of the local Democratic Party club (with instant coffee and supermarket cookies), several youth hostels, some Dominican *botánicas* with stylish religious art unknown to most New Yorkers, and a plethora of ethnic restaurants. One of the prettiest sections of Central Park is within walking distance.

Hoboken

The square mile city of Hoboken is nestled in a hidden corner of New Jersey. A few years ago, it lost its status as New York's best kept secret. Bordered by a high ridge to the west and the Hudson River to the east, Hoboken had no way to sprawl out, and thus retained the compactness necessary for strong community cohesion. Once an Italian neighborhood (Frank Sinatra was born here), Hoboken is now clearly multicultural, with a large contingent of Hispanic newcomers, Asians and some blacks. New York yuppies have discovered the place, and Hoboken is now a nightlife focal point. Conflicts between raucous after-hour drinkers and community traditionalists are being ironed out with the help of the hip priest, Father Michael Guglielmelli.

"Every block of Hoboken has its own personality," says Guglielmelli. "You can fit right in no matter how crazy you are."

Hoboken's lively street life and well-preserved brownstone architecture make it an attractive little city, only minutes from Battery Park and other points in Lower Manhattan by frequent ferries or by PATH (Port Authority Trans-Hudson) subway.

Hoboken has been the setting for dramatic films, such as Marlon Brando's classic *On The Waterfront* and several art movies by the alternative film master John Sayles, a Hoboken native. Just to the north, the equally compact city of Weehawken has many traits that are similar to Hoboken's.

Corona

You won't find this Queens neighborhood in any tourist books. It is unassuming, with rows of modest single-family homes and a few main arteries for daily commerce. I enjoyed this neighborhood because I was able to go to neighborhood bars where blacks and whites shared in fun and conversation. Both frequent flyers and Mets baseball fans might prefer this corner of New York. It's a hop and a skip from La Guardia Airport, and you can see the lights of Shea Stadium in the distance. A short bus ride will take you to more ethnic parts of Queens, and the 7 elevated line takes you to Manhattan.

HISTORY

Historians considering a work on New York City may choose from a variety of approaches . . .

Turf Wars

Those who see New York as a collection of distinct and changing neighborhoods might call their history "Turf Wars." Ever since the Dutch settled Manhattan in 1625 and "purchased" it a year later from the Indians for 60 Guilders ($24), New York's real estate has been changing hands—sometimes peacefully, other times with varying degrees of conflict.

On June 27, 1969, police raided the Stonewall Inn, a Greenwich Village bar on Christopher Street frequented by gay men. Such raids were commonplace, prompted by violations of liquor laws or failure to make police payoffs. Usually, patrons would prefer a quiet arrest rather than risking unflattering publicity. But patrons at the Stonewall Inn felt that the raid was but another example of police harassment of homosexuals, and they responded by attacking the police with rocks, bottles, and even a firebomb.

Greenwich Village had become a refuge of sorts for gays, and passersby showed their solidarity by joining the resistance, which extended to other parts of the Village and lasted for three nights. The block on Christopher Street where the bar stood is now named Stonewall Place.

In December 1986, three black youths got lost on "foreign turf" in the Howard Beach section of Brooklyn. When asking for directions, they stopped in a pizza parlor. When they emerged from the restaurant, they were chased by a gang of whites. During their escape, they attempted to cross an expressway. One of the youths was killed by an oncoming car. The Howard Beach defendants were eventually convicted and sentenced.

A list of other skirmishes based on defense of perceived turf would extend for pages. A more recent explosion involved tension between Hasidic Jews and blacks in the Crown Heights section of Brooklyn which led to a riot in 1991.

The New York City Police Department has not always been the good guy when entering the scene, as one Haitian immigrant who was sodomized by police while in custody can testify. The unflattering film *Serpico* was based on a true story of NYPD corruption. But by the late 1990s, New York had mellowed considerably, and many New Yorkers on the street now express gratitude for the added police protection provided by their municipal government. One wonders whether new turf wars are still simmering beneath the surface or if the city has somehow gotten past this part of her history.

Serial Criminals and Murderers

New York has had at least its fair share of bizarre criminals, although one could point out that other cities like Los Angeles, California are just as prone to such occurrences. The Mad Bomber (George P. Metesky) gained fame by planting 33 homemade bombs throughout New York City between 1940 and 1956. The Mad Bomber turned out to be a disgruntled electric company employee and was arrested at his home in Connecticut in 1957. He served 17 years in an asylum for the criminally insane until his release in 1974.

Another disgruntled public employee, David Berkowitz, known as Son of Sam, went on a murder spree between 1976 and 1977, shooting down five women and a man. His targets were young women seated in parked cars with male companions. Son of Sam courted publicity by signing his self-proclaimed nickname at the scenes of his crimes. He is now serving a 30-year sentence at the Attica prison in western New York State.

John Gotti was an organized crime leader who joined the Gambino crime family and was known as "Dapper Don." In 1985, he became head of the Gambino syndicate after ordering the assassination of its leader, Paul Castellano. Castellano was gunned down in front of Spark's Steak House in Midtown Manhattan. After various acquittals, Gotti was finally convicted and sentenced in 1992.

Such celebrity criminals earned considerable column inches in newspapers and magazines but had no ultimate impact on the city's history.

Immigration

A more significant approach to a history of the city would center around immigration. New Yorkers who currently gripe about escalating immigration would be surprised to learn that a 1911 Commission on Immigration found that in one major New York school district, three quarters of the students were foreign-born. Twenty-seven different nationalities were named in the study, including Finnish, Hebrew, and Syrian. In 1924, foreign-born New Yorkers made up 34 percent of the city's population. But that percentage dropped to 18 percent in 1970. Since then, thanks to more liberal immigration laws, the population of foreign-born New Yorkers has been steadily increasing.

Prior to 1970, the overwhelming majority of New York's immigrants were of European descent. Recent arrivals have come mainly from the Caribbean, South and East Asia, and the Middle East. Of the city's blacks, a half million come from the Caribbean. A quarter of the city's population is of Hispanic origin, and the half million Asians account for seven percent. There are more than 80 foreign-language or ethnic newspapers in the city. Korean greengrocers operate more than 80 percent of the city's produce stands.

When referring to violent incidents against immigrants, one must emphasize that a significant portion of New York's population applauds its mosaic of cultures and recognizes that the city is richer for it, both culturally and economically. Yes, racially-motivated murders and beatings of immigrants occasionally hit the headlines. But some anti-immigrant sentiment can be traced to a subtle system in which previous, more assimilated immigrants are pitted against more recent arrivals. The economic and social causes of this syndrome cannot be summarized and would require a polemical dissertation.

In July 1988, a group of Hispanics attacked Pakistanis who were worshipping at a Queens mosque. That same year saw a black-led boycott of Korean greengrocers in Brooklyn and Harlem, resulting from quarrels relating to claims of shoplifting on the one hand and claims of customer harassment on the other.

As immigration escalated, approximately 1 million whites left New York between 1970 and 1990, echoing the sentiment of a man interviewed by this author at a Queens swimming pool.

"I'm moving out of New York to Wisconsin," he said, "where I can live among real Americans."

His pronouncement mirrored a poll by the Empire Foundation and the Lehman Institute that found that a majority of city residents believed that too many immigrants were arriving and that these newcomers made the city a worse place to live. Yet during this same period of Third World immigration and white flight, New York's quality of life has improved by various statistical parameters, and the city's crime rate has gone down.

Economic statistics relating to race or national backgrounds can be confusing. On the one hand, the median income for blacks in Queens is higher than that of whites. But once immigrants (including Europeans) get through the first generation, their economy surpasses those New Yorkers who did not come here on their own will. The overall average income of non-immigrant African Americans is next to last, with Puerto Ricans at the bottom. For one Puerto Rican, what seemed complex to me was obvious to him.

"We're here not as immigrants," he said, "but because we are a colony of the United States. Like African-Americans, but unlike immigrants, we have been stripped of our national identity. This creates internal psychological barriers.

"Look at the Southwest. Why do recent Mexican immigrants often do better economically than Chicanos who've been here for centuries? Why are Native Americans, who were colonized, at the bottom of the economic totem pole?"

Social Thought
Any history of New York based on social thinkers would have to begin with Jacob Riis. Originally from Denmark, Riis became a police reporter for the *New York Tribune* in the 1870s. Riis took photographs of the filth and degradation of New York's slums, typically called tenements. He became an advocate for immigrants

41

and his photo essays made the middle class confront the reality of poverty.

In the 1920s and 1930s, the Harlem Renaissance showcased the glorious creative powers of leading black writers, musicians, and artists. The poetry of Langston Hughes and Ralph Ellison's *Invisible Man* are must-reading for the images and perceptions of the period.

In the 1950s, the "beat" writers in Greenwich Village, including Jack Kerouac and Allen Ginsburg, developed an anarchist, anti-puritanical philosophy that would influence a whole generation. But strangely, most of these writers abandoned New York for California. Among other important writers to become self-exiles from New York were Alice Walker, who moved to California, and James Baldwin, who found his peace in France.

In the 1960s, New York's history of social thought would take a quantum leap with the imposing presence of Malcolm X. Not since Kerouac was my youth so influenced by any figure. I would go to Union Square to hear and sometimes participate in debates with the Black Muslims, often as the only white kid in the crowd. The theme of some of the debates was whether or not white people were inherently evil.

As a kid I'd listen to Malcolm on the radio. This former petty criminal turned intellectual and nationalist leader denounced Martin Luther King's pacifism and integration, arguing instead for black community control. But his flaming rhetoric was distinct from his actions, and I felt safer amidst a group of Black Muslims than I did in certain white neighborhoods of my city.

One aspect of Malcolm X's life that is underemphasized in *The Autobiography of Malcolm X* (by Alex Haley) is his conversion from nationalist to internationalist following his visits to Africa. Malcolm X had become a spokesman for Third World peoples, and perhaps this universality led to his being placed under surveillance by the federal government. Years later, his oldest daughter was a student of mine, and she corroborated my belief that Malcolm X had become a spokesman for all oppressed peoples, even if they happened to be white.

On the 14th of February in 1965, Malcolm's house was firebombed. A week later, while he was giving an address at the Audobon Ballroom in Manhattan, he was shot to death. I was too immature at the time to analyze the meaning of his death. Whether the real intellectual authors of his murder have been identified is a matter of debate, but over the years I have been increasingly convinced that he was murdered not because of his nationalism but because of his internationalism.

Other important figures in New York's social history have followed, but none with such impact as Malcolm X. As a center of intellectual life, New York offers too many important names to mention here. For a view of New York in the 1980s, Tom Wolfe's novel *The Bonfire of the Vanities*, Spike Lee's film *Do the Right Thing*, and Robert DeNiro's *Bronx Story* are highly recommended.

ROBERT MOSES AND ME

Who really ruled New York? At various points in the city's history one could argue about the comparative power of the Rockefeller family, the Tammany Hall political machine, and the crime syndicate. But one man, whose presence towered over a series of mayors he supposedly worked for, has had a lasting impact on this city, and coincidentally on my own life.

Between the end of World War II and 1953, Robert Moses, as the head of the Triborough Bridge and Tunnel Authority, oversaw the most intense construction in the history of New York, of parkways, expressways, bridges, parks, and beaches. Thousands of citizens were evicted from homes and apartments under eminent domain laws to make way for Robert Moses projects.

Throughout a career that spanned several decades, Moses's antipathy for buses and railroad trains bordered on strange vengeance, as if he'd been hit by a bus in his childhood. The under-passes over his earliest highways were intentionally made too low for buses to pass underneath, even though an express bus with 40 passengers would have been so much more ecologically sensible than 40 separate passenger cars.

No matter which mayor was in power at the time, Moses refused to plan for inexpensive mass transit right-of-way areas in the center medians of his expressway projects. In fact, between the end of World War II and 1960 alone, agencies under the domination of Moses spent nearly five billion dollars, not a penny of which went to public transportation.

The automobiles required to transport the equivalent of a single trainload of commuters would use approximately four acres of parking space in Manhattan! As kids, we were too immature intellectually to challenge such folly, and in the 1960s, I remember believing that my economics professor, Mr. Foster, was crazy to believe that "trains will make a comeback."

In 1959, when my beloved Brooklyn Dodgers moved to Los Angeles, I assumed the entire blame rested on owner Walter O'Malley. But years later, I learned that O'Malley had offered to put up $5 million for a new stadium in downtown Brooklyn. O'Malley was told by none other than Robert Moses that the new stadium would create "a China wall of traffic." Of course, Moses would have never considered a simple system of shuttle buses from various Brooklyn subway stops as the answer to the traffic problem.

I was still too young to understand that my father, as a leader and participant in community organizations, was taking up a struggle against the all-powerful Moses, opposing a second deck above the Long Island Expressway (which goes all the way from outer Long Island to the mouth of the Midtown Tunnel under the East River), and organizing against a bridge to be built across the Long Island Sound from Connecticut.

After reading Robert Caro's Pulitzer Prize-winning *The Power Broker: Robert Moses and the Fall of New York* (1974), I now realize that anyone opposing Moses, including my father, had to be nothing less than heroic. Both the Connecticut-to-Long Island bridge and the second deck of the Expressway were defeated by public activism, but not until most of Robert Moses's damage had been done.

In September of 1998, my 13-year-old son Marcus and I arrived at La Guardia Airport. We should have been on time to see the New York's baseball Mets final home game. The Mets were in a three-way race for the final post-season play-off berth, so it was going to be the most important game of the season.

Our plane was late, and by the time Marcus and I could dump our suitcases in a hotel near the airport, several innings of the night game had already been played. We were within a short distance of Shea Stadium. Rather than waiting for public transportation we decided to take what should have been no more than a 20-minute walk to Shea Stadium.

We decided to fast-walk it with occasional sprints through the warm, humid air. After five minutes, we saw the stadium lights glaring in our eyes and we knew we'd make it for the final exciting innings. But we hadn't bargained on Robert Moses's restructuring of this important part of the city. We could practically reach out and touch the stadium, and yet three expressways and/or lengthy overpasses stood in our way.

The street signs all said "SHEA STADIUM." If cars can get to the stadium from here, I thought, there must be a way for a pedestrian as well. But once we began crossing the highway maze, the stadium was not getting any closer. We took a left for about 300 meters, then hopped over a highway barrier only to end up on another expressway, which turned right for another 300 meters. All we needed to do was to go straight ahead, but that would mean a fifty meter jump to the ground.

A roar from the stadium suggested that someone had hit a home run, and we had missed it because of Robert Moses's expressway madness. Moses had something to do with the treason of my Dodgers, and now he was preventing me from seeing the Mets. We finally arrived during the seventh inning.

The Mets lost the game and didn't make the play-offs. But recently, New York's public transportation system has become more efficient and offers more alternatives for those of us who would prefer to take a train or a bus (see Chapter 3). Oddly enough, Robert Moses never drove his own car.

WEATHER REPORT

Even if the geographical, social, and historical settings were perfect, some potential visitors would demand a comfortable climate as well. Does New York pass your test? Here are the facts. You decide.

Most of my ex-New Yorker friends in California have longed for the change of seasons of their hometown. New York has four distinct seasons, two of which (spring and autumn) would pass the test of the most demanding judges. Spring's sweet, temperate weather, with refreshing rains and burgeoning aromas, is hard to beat. The more melancholy "Autumn in New York" deservedly inspired one of the great all-time songs. In mid-October and early November, New Yorkers often depart for upstate or New England to partake of the colorful transformation of the foliage to leaves of bright yellows, oranges, burgundies and reds. But New York City's foliage changes to exuberant colors as well, and the city's leafy parks offer romantic spots to contemplate the dying foliage on a nippy autumn day. As late as November, the city and suburbs may experience what is called "Indian Summer" which often preludes the first taste of winter.

When compared to other U.S. cities at the same latitude, New York's winters are relatively mild, and its summers not as muggy as one would expect. New York's mean January tempera-ture of 31.5°F is considerably higher than Chicago's 21.0°F. During the month of January, the cities of Portland (Oregon), Boston, Detroit, St. Louis, Cleveland, Pittsburgh, and Salt Lake City are all colder than New York.

New York's midsummer July mean temperature of 76.8°F is lower than that of Washington, D.C. (80.0°F), Dallas (82.3°F), Miami (82.6°F), and other southern cities, and New Yorkers are spared the steamy excesses of Midwest heat binges. But a heat spell with high humidity can make New York's dog days quite uncomfortable, sending citizens into their air-conditioned refuges. Air conditioning has become a necessity for the large majority of New Yorkers. But nights tend to cool off, with an average mini-mum July temperature of 68.4°F, perfect for Shakespeare in the Park or a Yankee night game.

Among major U.S. cities, New York ranks 27th in the amount of annual precipitation, with 0.01 inches or more of rain, snow, or sleet cleansing the air (or spoiling a picnic, depending on how you see it) on 121 days of the year. The good news is that New York's parks and gardens do not rely on irrigation. New York's natural green, I tell my ex-New Yorker California friends, does not depend of massive and unsustainable movement of water from hundreds of miles away to create the illusion that the southern California desert is a green paradise.

Once you know you can handle the weather, the next step is to deal with the people, not a simple matter, but rewarding if you can make the right human adjustments.

Chapter Two

THEY BARK BUT DO THEY BITE?
(Getting Along with New Yorkers)

In my country, government rules are not as strong as they are here, but there we have social rules. Here, government rules try to help. There, if you are suffering from sorrow, people come to you. Here, there is no one.

—Bangladeshi immigrant, Lower East Side

Having been raised in New York, my greatest apprehension about writing a book about my hometown was the possibility of missing the obvious. When we look at our own culture, we risk taking things for granted, or worse, ignoring certain aspects of reality that would have an impact on outsiders.

To partially compensate for my hometown handicap, I made sure my 13-year-old son Marcus, not a New Yorker, would undertake the role of outsider. He had lived in southern California, Maryland, France, and South America, and for him, New York was like a foreign place.

"Why do so many New Yorkers cuss and argue out on the street in front of other people?" he asked. After a few days he'd witnessed more than a few public disputes, including heated verbal altercation in a line at a post office and a loud argument over a chess match in Washington Square. Only in New York could a chess match be treated as prize fight. A real New Yorker, wrote Laermer, "can take an argument about pizza seriously."

Within a week, Marcus had heard the world's most popular four-letter word more often than in his previous 13 years.

New Yorkers have no monopoly on being verbally pugnacious and rough-edged, with or without the trimmings of the

Washington Square chess regulars take their games very seriously.

49

f-word, but some visitors jump to the false conclusion that what they hear is what they get.

Sophisticated outsiders enjoy identifying this perceived obstinacy with sardonic understatement. At an academic convention in Las Vegas, Nevada, one New Yorker attending the event, whom we shall call R, had haughtily insulted his colleagues when dealing with one of the polemics of their field.

The whole conference was on the brink of deteriorating into a petty dispute. It was the verbal equivalent of an ice hockey game evolving into a brawl. That evening, at a banquet, the guest speaker (a Californian) tried to ease the stress by declaring that R. would receive the "Ed Koch award for diplomacy." (Koch, inveterate New Yorker and former mayor, was known for his verbal belligerence.)

Yet, with all of New York's bellicose verbosity, the rates of murder and violent crime in more mellow Los Angeles, California and in various proper, good-mannered southern cities are considerably higher than in New York. The same verbal confrontation that in New York may end with renewed friendship, may lead a violent denouement in other parts of the country.

New Yorkers can dish it out effortlessly, but they can also take it in stride.

INDIVIDUALISM

Most visitors soon learn to tolerate the verbal aggressiveness of some but not all New Yorkers. But more enigmatic is how to break through barriers of individualism. Metro International, a non-profit organization dedicated to helping foreign students and scholars adjust to New York explains this "individualism inherent in U.S. culture" as "the need to constantly make decisions for oneself," which becomes a challenge for newcomers from more collectively-oriented societies in which decision-making is often a social matter, and asking for help, or offering it, is a norm.

My experience narrows down this propensity for individual decision-making to a regional phenomenon most typical of New York and the northeastern coast. This author once did a study on selection services for legal sports and horse racing wagering. I was surprised to discover that Californians were more likely to subscribe to such services while their counterparts in New York didn't think any "expert" would know more than they did, and were thus less likely to subscribe. Indeed, New Yorkers represented a far greater proportion of the purveyors of such information than "touts" from other parts of the country. At least within this information-oriented activity, New Yorkers prefer to provide opinions rather than receive them.

This and other aspects of individualism make it difficult for newcomers to mingle with and get to know native New Yorkers. Foreigners sometimes perceive this individualism as callousness.

"In my country," a Bangladeshi photography shop owner in the East Village told this reporter, "government rules are not as strong as they are here, but there we have social rules. Here the government tries to help. There, if you are suffering from sorrow, people come to you. Here there is no one."

A Colombian student agreed with the Bangladeshi, adding that in his country there is "street life," while in New York no one speaks on the street.

Surveying foreign student advisors at major New York universities, I wanted to know what were the most typical difficulties in adjusting to New York. Two obstacles dominated in their answers: finding housing (a problem that can be worked out with the right strategy; see Chapter 4) and getting to know New Yorkers. Both the individualism of New Yorkers and the fast pace of life were mentioned as friendship barriers.

"International students often find it difficult to motivate Americans to take an interest in their own home countries and cultures" and "meeting people and friends can be difficult," especially monocultural Americans.

At one English-language school, many foreign students say they "want to meet Americans but don't know how," according to a teacher.

What they do not understand about the United States in general and New York in particular is that friendships usually do not form within a community among neighbors, as they would in some traditional cultures. Friendships emerge out of work relationships and common interests that draw people together.

Finding friends is not simply a dilemma for foreigners. The large section of personal ads in *The Village Voice* are replete with yearnings for human contact. Foreign newcomers might be surprised to learn that most of these ads (and I'm not referring to the ones that hunt for a sexual partner) come from natives of the United States including New Yorkers themselves.

Clearly, modern alienation is not simply a function of place, and may have much to do with transformations from traditional communities to a so-called global culture, and the technological innovations that seduce people to remain at home. Within New York, one is more likely to find cohesive traditional communities than in many other great cities. But once one has passed the invisible barrier from the traditional way of life of our Bangladeshi friend to a more universal existence, new paradigms for companionship emerge.

Researchers at Carnegie Mellon University expected that the Internet—with its accessible chat rooms for interactive communication, would serve to diminish the type of depression associated with loneliness. But their two-year study found just the opposite.

"People who spend even a few hours a week on line experience higher levels of depression and loneliness than if they used the computer network less frequently," according to the study.

In New York, fitting in with other people is further complicated by a scenario in which more than 100 ethnic groups and "statuspheres" come into contact and then separate (John Tierney's "parallel lives in New York" theory revisited).

It is not the objective of this book to engage in sociological analysis of modern alienation. Newcomers to New York want practical tips for how to fit in and get involved socially with New Yorkers. What follows then is a pragmatic strategy for penetrating the apparent layer of indifference and finding what I believe is the city's inherent humanity.

SIX WAYS TO *NOT* MEET NEW YORKERS

1. **Visit the Statue of Liberty, the World Trade Center and a Broadway show.** According to Laermer, the real New Yorker "has never been to the Statue of Liberty or the World Trade Center observation deck." The first and only time I visited the Statue of Liberty was at the age of 25, when a houseguest from South America insisted I take him there.

2. **Try to see as much of the city as possible in the shortest possible time.** I call this the walking encyclopedia syndrome, in which a tourist feels that he or she must see everything to know a place. Consider that if you are constantly on the move, a sense of place and the people who are part of it will pass by like a fast blur.

3. **Stay in a hotel.** No building in the history of cultures is so alienating as a hotel. Most native New Yorkers have never stayed in a hotel in their own city. Why should they? Anything else with four walls is better than a hotel. You're more likely to meet other New Yorkers in a jail cell than in a hotel room.

4. **Follow the advice of your travel agent.** The job of travel agents is to get people in and out of places with no mishaps. No mishap means avoiding uncertainties. If you avoid all uncertainties, I promise you will emerge from New York safe

and free from the plague of other human beings. A tour bus will keep you in the presence of other tourists. In the subway, though, you might meet your future mate, or the Mad Bomber.

5. **Avoid arguments at all costs.** Certain traditional cultures, even within the United States, avoid verbal confrontation. In some parts of the United States, an argument might spell the end of a friendship. But New Yorkers tend to enjoy polemics, and not participating in an argument might mean being left out of a conversation. Your opinion is part of your individuality. Don't express it and you remain anonymous.

6. **Drive a car wherever you go.** Whether you drive alone or are accompanied by someone you already know, an automobile will insulate you from bumping into other people. Only by crashing into another car will you have the chance to meet someone else. You could also pick up a hitchhiker—in the 1950s, a lucky driver had a shot at picking up Jack Kerouac.

NINE WAYS TO BECOME INVOLVED WITH NEW YORKERS

People from the United States often relate to each other as occupants of roles rather than as whole people. They will know you as a chess player, a skydiver, a legal secretary, a baseball fan. People tend to get together around common interests. The following annotated list will dramatically increase your probability of becoming involved with New Yorkers.

1. **Take a non-credit continuing education course.** Suppose that you choose a course in gardening. You've got a 100 percent probability that everyone else in the classroom will be interested in the same subject. On the other hand, you've got about a tenth of one percent chance that the guy next to you in the subway loves gardening as much as you do. New York has an amazing array of continuing (or adult) education classes. (See Interactive Directory.)

2. **Choose a neighborhood that most fits with your affinities, and do your daily commerce with the same merchants.** In this way, people will get to know you and in turn, you will become aware of the most pressing local concerns. Trying a different fruit stand and pizza place every time you do errands might be fascinating but it will also help to maintain your anonymity. By regularly patronizing a ma-and-pa grocery, you will get to know a ma and pa.

3. **Become a volunteer.** New York needs you. As a by-product of volunteer work, you will be sharing a common objective with other committed individuals. *Volunteering in New York City: Your Guide to Working Small Miracles in the Big Apple* by Richard Mintzer offers a treasury of volunteer opportunities and is found in most New York bookstores. Local phone numbers of volunteer agencies are listed in the Interactive Directory.

4. **Become active in community issues.** Once you've chosen a neighborhood, you will become aware that the residents have certain needs that will probably be your needs as well. Community organizations can use all the help they can get. Your presence will be appreciated.

5. **Share an apartment.** Apartment-sharing agencies are advertised in newspapers like the *Voice* and *The New York Press* and just about every other city and community paper with a classified ads section. With New York's high housing costs, sharing has become a major alternative, and agencies dealing in apartment or house sharing have become quite sophisticated in matching house mates. Caution: there is a certain degree of risk involved, but the ultimate choice is yours once a potential sharer is presented to you. You may prefer the less formal route of consulting the bulletin board of a church, volunteer, community, or recreational organization where you are already known. (For more on apartment sharing, see Chapter 4 on housing.)

6. **Organize a research project before you arrive in New York.** The newspaper in your hometown, your university, or your professional organization may want information about New York. If so, they may supply you with a press credential or a letter of introduction that would allow you to open doors that would normally be off limits to a stranger.

7. **Get a job.** Friendships in the United States often originate in the work place. Many New Yorkers are more driven by their professions than by leisure interests, and they can't wait to get back to work after a vacation. Working in a goal-oriented craft or profession with other people is a source of fraternal solidarity. This may seem very obvious, but today's work world is increasingly populated by self-employed people or those who are linked electronically to their company's office from their homes. This may be one of the reasons for the proliferation of personal ads in search of relationships. What you need is an old-fashioned workplace where people still share the burdens of work.

8. **Join a professional or recreational organization or sports team.** For those workers who have no daily contact with their peers (small business people and free lance contractors), a professional organization provides human contact based on affinities. Likewise, hobbyists would do well to link up with their peers through recreational organizations. Reference sections of public libraries carry the *Encyclopedia of Associations* and other reference books with names and contact numbers of those local organizations with open admission. (See Interactive Directory for sports activities.)

9. **Choose a social club with "your own kind."** This solution may represent a cop-out, since one of New York's main attractions is its diversity. I also believe that a baseball player from Santo Domingo has more in common with a baseball player from Brooklyn than with a telephone technician from Santo Domingo. A chess player from Italy should have more in common with a chess player from Washington Square than with a soap opera addict from Italy.

A Mix That Matches

I hope I'm dead wrong about the "finding your own kind" strategy, but New York's reality presents evidence of night clubs that are integrated during the first two sets of music only to become segregated after hours when people really begin to relate to each other. I've seen Mexican workers who might have little in common with each other back in Mexico drink beers together after work and then return to an apartment building inhabited by all Mexicans.

Students in English classes for foreigners want desperately to meet "Americans," but they often live in neighborhoods where there are few native New Yorkers. If a segregated neighborhood is not to blame, then it's what one foreign student calls "the hectic way of life" in which one goes from a difficult job back home to sleep, and then begins preparing for work again at the crack of dawn. Missing is the traditional big midday meal with family and friends. Missing are the improvised visits from neighbors. Missing are informal community gathering places.

ETHNIC GROUPS . . . AND OTHER FRAGMENTS OF NEW YORK'S IMAGINATION

Between a third and a half of New York's population was born outside the city. According to John Tierney, "Manhattan has the highest concentration of single-person households in America except for an island in Hawaii settled as a leper colony."

As a specialist in Latin American cultures, I perceive that Mexicans in Queens, Dominicans in Washington Heights, and Puerto Ricans in El Barrio carry on their lives on distinct channels. Even living within blocks of each other, African Americans and Caribbean blacks maintain separate ways of life. Working-class whites and white members of the publishing and arts communities seem eons apart.

Some New York social critics believe that no other city has collected such a wide array of strangers, although Los Angeles might vie for the same distinction, and Washington, D.C. seems far more polarized to me than New York. Why such alienation exists is a matter of conjecture. Marxists believe that social fragmentation is the result of subtle, almost unconscious attempts by a ruling class to divide and therefore conquer. People who are struggling for survival and who have so many common social and economic goals cannot fight for their rights if they are alienated from each other. Meanwhile, some humanists believe that New York's intrinsic loneliness (and not a class conspiracy) drives people to find refuge with their own kind.

Still others argue that such social divisions result from an economic system based on rigid commercial niches. Italian restaurants, for example, now mirror the regions of Italy, so that northern and southern Italians might find themselves on different channels. Hasidic and secular Jews are worlds apart. As we've noted, New York's social fragmentation is most evident at after-hour social clubs, which allow an otherwise mixed society to create extended ethnic families that compensate for the lack of real extended families.

A comparison between New York and Paris is appropriate at this juncture. Paris too has its multiethnic components, as could be visualized with the rainbow of ethnic backgrounds of players on the 1998 World Cup championship team (with origins in France, the Caribbean, Africa, and the Arabic world). While in New York, each fragment of music lovers has its own neatly delineated musical niche, in Paris a *musique metisse* has developed. Sometimes it's difficult to define whether a particular Parisian music is from the Caribbean, West Africa, black U.S.A., or France itself. French musicians of Arabic origin perform music that resembles hip hop. And native French people participate in performing and listening to this musical melting pot.

New York, on the other hand, has a plethora of neatly defined musical niches having little "crossover," which means few crosscultural musical experiences.

The divide-and-conquer theory seems relevant when comparing New York's ailing labor movement to Paris's strike-happy workers. But humanists argue that Parisian labor unrest has historical-cultural roots unrelated to manipulation by any ruling class.

The ideal of a rainbow coalition is far from the reality of New York. But certain crosscultural pockets within the city keep the flame of crosscultural and international understanding aglow. New York City is the world capital of international education. A number of crosscultural organizations in New York strive to nurture an internationalist spirit that coexists with the city's ethnic fragmentation. One of them is here portrayed.

METRO INTERNATIONAL

Metro International is a private, non-profit membership organization which links New York City with the rest of the world through a variety of educational services and outreach programs. Dedicated to promoting global understanding, this idealistic organization creates opportunities for cultural, social, and intellectual exchange between 40,000 international students enrolled at New York-area campuses and residents of the metropolitan area.

New York's 7 percent foreign enrollment in higher education more than doubles the national average. With the $7 billion per year that international students and their family members spend on tuition and living expenses, higher education becomes the sixth largest U.S. export industry. In the 1995-96 academic year, international students contributed $1.2 billion to the economy of New York State!

Chinese student volunteer in Metro International's Global Classroom program

Metro International serves these students by providing cultural tours; homestays; revealing visits to social, cultural, and political institutions; and publications helping visitors settle in New York. One of Metro International's goals is to bridge the gap between foreigners and native New Yorkers through a number of joint activities. Metro's Global Classroom program deserves special mention. In this program, visiting foreign students do volunteer presentations in inner city schools.

Another trailblazing program, "Corporate Visits," involves mini-internships pairing foreign business personnel with their American counterparts.

According to Margaret Shiba, Metro International's dynamic executive director, "Students don't have to be enrolled at a Metro member institution to register for our programs." Foreign students doing internships with New York companies are also welcomed. For more information on this crosscultural organization, write to: 285 West Broadway, Suite 450, New York, NY 10013 (or check Metro's website at *http://www.metrointl.org*).

Metro International's advice to newcomers who wish to interact socially with New Yorkers:

"Take the initiative yourself; say hello; call and keep calling; reach out and take a risk; don't sit home waiting for the phone to ring. Show an interest in other people; look for a common ground on which to build a conversation."

IN DEFENSE OF NEW YORKERS

Breaking through the social barriers of New York is indeed difficult. But once you get through, there is no guess work. In other parts of the country and the world, the newcomer is kept guessing about the intentions of new acquaintances. What some outsiders call the New Yorker's bluntness, I see as honesty. I also affirm, after having lived in four other U.S. cities, that in New York and among New Yorkers, there has been a greater sense of fairness towards the less fortunate than in most other parts of the country. New York's remarkable variety of volunteer organizations backs up my claim.

There is also another side to the coin of New York's lack of cohesiveness. In the absence of the social rules so very much missed by our Pakistani friend, there is a tolerance for people who are different, for people who have trouble following social codes. It is easier to be a nonconformist in New York than in most parts of the world.

CHAPTER THREE

GETTING AROUND

*I'm from Oklahoma but I just moved here from southern California.
I have my car. But when I experienced the traffic and the parking
fees, I decided I'm going to sell my car and take the subway.*
— Woman on the New York subway

"What would be the most important comment you could make to
your friends about New York?" I asked my son Marcus.

"How easy it is to get around," he answered.

Like the woman from Oklahoma, Marcus had been raised
in an automobile culture, and in our other cities we had used
public transportation sparingly, depending mainly on our car. He
had experienced the luxury of hopping into a car and being driven
to wherever he wanted to go. And yet, here in New York,
hopping into a subway seemed so much more efficient to him —
and more pleasant.

He had not experienced the New York subway system when it was riddled with graffiti, nor when certain stations were scenarios of nightly horror stories.

TALE OF A SUBWAY VIGILANTE

In 1984, three days before Christmas, four black youths approached Bernard Goetz, a 37-year-old electronics engineer, in the Chambers Street station in Lower Manhattan and asked him for money. (When confronted with a similar situation, also in a Lower Manhattan station—although the accosters were white—my frightened but quick-thinking friend Frank, a writer and musician, began to howl, moan, and mutter like many of the deranged men you find in New York subways. Frank's artistry paid off. His potential accosters fled.)

But Mr. Goetz, unaccustomed to artistic solutions to human problems, drew an unlicensed handgun and fired at all four youths—one of whom, Darrel Cabey, became paralyzed and brain-damaged as a result of the shooting.

The acts of the subway vigilante became the focus of international debate. To some, Goetz was a hero against urban crime, but to others, he was a depraved vigilante motivated by racism. In his 1987 trial, Goetz was acquitted of attempted murder but sentenced to a year plus five years' probation for illegal possession of a handgun. He served eight months on Rikers Island.

Newcomers who know the New York subways only from the Goetz story will be burdened with unwarranted anxiety.

YOUR DECISION

One of the major decisions facing visitors to New York is whether to ride or drive. Short-term visitors must grapple with the choice between renting a car and using the public transportation services provided by New York's **Metropolitan Transportation Authority (MTA)**. Those who arrive for a long stay will need to decide whether it is in their interest to purchase an automobile, and if so, how often to use it.

I have spent years both driving in New York and as a regular user of public transportation. I shall present the alternatives in as objective a manner as possible. Though my persuasions will become apparent, you will have enough information to make a decision based on your own needs and lifestyle.

SUBWAYS

Most New Yorkers refer to the subway and its elevated lines (or "els") as "the train," but to avoid confusion with other commuter trains and Amtrak, we'll call it what it is. By 1997, crime within subways and other transit systems in Manhattan had declined significantly. The obvious cause for such an improvement in safety is linked to greater police presence in subways and on buses. But New York's improved economy, generated by rising stocks on Wall Street and a flourishing tourist industry, may have had something to do with the drop in crime statistics.

Mexican musicians entertain subway passengers. Give them a tip.

Good to have this guy on your side when you ride the subway.

Between 1997 and 1998, further improvements were noted. In 1997, a single murder took place within Manhattan's transit system. In 1998, the figure was reduced to zero. Other crime statistics mirrored the decline between 1997 and 1998, although one is advised to be street smart at all times when using public transportation. Approximately 500 robberies were committed within the system in Manhattan alone in 1998.

That figure may seem alarming until you consider that millions of people use public transportation on a daily basis. If you have a choice between Manhattan's east side or west side lines, crime statistics are higher on the east side. Gene Russianoff, staff attorney for the Straphangers Campaign, a subway users' advocacy group, labels the Times Square station as the most dangerous.

"The busiest/ugliest station in the world is Times Square," he writes. "It's a disgrace . . . it's Disneyland above and hell below."

But Russianoff grudgingly admits that even many of the worst stations are improving. In reference to the passageway between Times Square and the Port Authority Bus Terminal, he notes that, "It's not Dante's Inferno like it used to be, but there's room for improvement."

Along with added police, subway stations are being adorned with attractive mosaic art, with the wall murals in each station referring to the history of the neighborhood above.

Once you become a regular user of the subway system, you will learn to increase your safety percentages. The later it gets at night, the less time you want to spend waiting on platforms. Stations with no transfer lines are more likely to have deserted platforms late at night. Choose stations in which the exit is nearest to the train platform, even if it means walking an extra block or two above ground. Learn which car of the train will leave you off exactly at the platform exit, surprisingly easy to master once you know your regular routes. Remain alert at all times, and if possible, travel accompanied. At night, use the middle cars which will be carrying more passengers. (During the day, end cars provide the greatest probability of getting a seat.)

The graffiti's gone and in its place is some flashy mosaic subway art.

67

Statistically it's probably safer to take the subway than to drive a car in the city, and subways are recognized as the quickest way to get from one part of the city to another.

Subway tokens cost $1.50 per ride, with free transfers when tunneling from one line to another. But few people pay the flat rate. Unless you're in the city for a day, it's best to purchase a **MetroCard**™, a debit card good for use on both subways and buses. MetroCards are available in all subway stations and in more than 3,600 neighborhood stores. Senior citizens and people with disabilities are granted special reduced fares.

Formulae and prices may vary, but the following 1999 rates will illustrate the savings of a MetroCard versus pay-per-ride. A 7-Day Unlimited Ride MetroCard costs $17. During this seven-day period, if you plan to ride a subway and/or bus more than 11 times, the MetroCard represents consumer savings. For example, if you're living in Queens and need to take a bus to your train in order to get to work, that's already four rides during the day, and 20 for the workweek. With so much happening through-out the city on weekends, you will be going out and about with your MetroCard in hand; add another eight weekend rides and you've got 28 rides for $17. That's about 60 cents per ride, as opposed to $1.50 on a pay-per-ride basis.

It gets better with the 30-Day MetroCard for $63. Only a hermit or agoraphobe will do better with the pay-per-ride system. And these cards also cover the **MTA Staten Island Railroad**, the **MTA Long Island Bus**, and most private bus lines.

You can also buy Pay-Per-Ride MetroCards in denominations of $3 to $80. This system is good for people who transfer from subways to buses, since subway-to-bus, bus-to-subway, and bus-to-bus transportation is free within two hours when you use the card. Even a $15 MetroCard is valuable, since it includes an extra ride for free, and also does not charge for transfers to buses within two hours.

Once you have your card, you merely swipe it at the turn-stile entrance, or on the bus, so ticket booth hassles are gone. For getting around, even those who consider themselves map-illiterate will find it easy to use the free subway and bus maps.

If this sounds like an advertisement for the MTA, so be it. The system works.

BUSES

Folks who choose to reside near a subway line will have little need for buses. But some of the best housing bargains, both for renting and buying, are beyond subway lines. You may end up saving money on housing only to exhaust your savings on the automobile you now need because you decided on a "bargain" rent away from a subway line.

Or, you may use the bus-subway combination for getting to work or reaching entertainment destinations. If this is the case, it would be imperative to purchase a 7-Day or 30-Day MetroCard, which will more than compensate for the absence of bus-to-subway transfers.

Most New York buses are slow, but are strategically used as connections with subway lines. One of various exceptions is the **M60 bus**, which will whisk you from upper Broadway at either 106th or 116th Street all the way to La Guardia Airport in about 45 minutes, depending on the time of day. For other express and semi-express buses, call 718-330-1234.

The majority of bus drivers are extremely courteous, with a few who behave as if you're there to bother them. One driver offered us an unsolicited free ride when he learned we were on our way to the subway to purchase a MetroCard. Exact change ($1.50 at this writing) is required for pay-per-ride bus trips. Most U.S. city bus systems take bills, but New York buses require coins. It's not unusual to see people board the bus and then ask other riders for change.

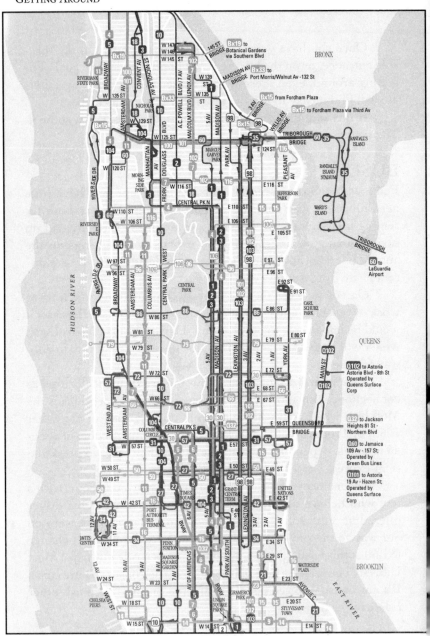

(Lower Manhattan continues at the top of the next page)

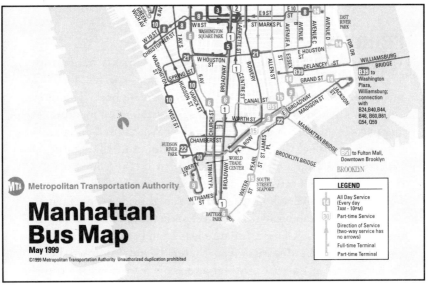

® 1998 New York City Transit Authority

Maps

Free MTA subway and bus maps are available at any subway station booth (as well as hotel information desks and tourist information stands). The maps are easy to use, and, in the unlikely case that you become confused about a route, you may call 718-330-1234 for guidance. (Non-English speakers can call 718-330-4847.) The most universal source of transportation information in New York City is **The Map®**, which indicates subway, ferry, and commuter-train lines, plus strategic bus lines and transfer points. Every phone number you'll ever need to know about public transportation in New York is listed on this handy (and free) map.

For strictly bus routes, get yourself a free copy of the MTA **Manhattan Bus Map®** (shown above and opposite), which not only shows all Manhattan bus service details, but also lists the addresses and relevant bus/subway services for major landmarks, museums, libraries, and transportation hubs. (Note: the Manhattan Bus Map shown is current as of May 1999 and is subject to change. Reprinted with the permission of the MTA.)

71

FERRIES

The famous **Staten Island Ferry**, once known as a bargain for 5 cents, and later at 25 cents, is now a free ride—perfect for Wall Street brokers who can afford their own private boat. The ferry doubles as a commuter vehicle and an entertainment medium, as it departs from Battery Park, just south of Wall Street, and passes between the sleek-lined Verrazano Bridge and the Statue of Liberty on its course to Staten Island. It will take your car for a fee. The ferry operates every half hour between 6:30 a.m. and 11:30 p.m., and every hour thereafter. A night ride is spectacular.

Other privately-owned ferries, sometimes twice as fast as the Staten Island "Classic," charge fees from between $3 and $15 depending on the distance. The Staten Island-Midtown Ferry drops you off at East 34th Street and provides you with a transfer. New Jersey commuters can choose between the various New Jersey-to-New York ferries, or the **PATH (Port Authority Trans-Hudson)** subway for a dollar.

You can even find ferries that will take you to La Guardia Airport or Yankee Stadium.

COMMUTER RAILROADS

Commuters to Long Island, Westchester County, Connecticut, or New Jersey, enjoy comfortable railroad service. **MTA Metro-North Railroad** services Westchester and other New York State counties farther north, as well as Fairfield and farther-east Connecticut counties, out of the elegantly refurbished **Grand Central Terminal** (42nd Street). **MTA-Long Island Rail Road** commuters reach their final Manhattan terminal at **Penn Station** (34th Street). New Jersey commuters from north of Hudson Country use New Jersey Transit rail lines and end up at the **Hoboken Terminal**, where they must then take the ferry or PATH to get to Manhattan.

PRIVATE AUTOMOBILES

A large majority of users of commuter railroads reside in communities where it is indispensable to own an automobile. They have the choice of driving to Manhattan or using the train. Even with the cost of train rides, which is prorated according to the distance, they choose to leave their cars at home. Parking and bridge or tunnel tolls to Manhattan would be more expensive yet, and rush hour traffic usually cancels out any time that would have been saved by driving. On the train they read newspapers, do work, or just relax.

Pros and Cons of Owning and Using an Automobile

If you are from Europe, you'll easily understand why such a discussion is necessary. But if you are coming to New York from most other cities in the United States, where an automobile is an indispensable icon, you'll wonder why there's any discussion at all.

In Favor

Having an automobile allows you more housing options. Especially if you prefer the comfort of a larger residence as a trade-off for being away from "the action," you'll most likely end up in a community where you need a car.

The legend of stressful driving in New York — and especially in Manhattan — is overblown. After this writer drove regularly in Mexico City, Manhattan seemed apt for amateur drivers. If your driving plans cover non-rush hour times, traffic on expressways and through bridges and tunnels usually flows more smoothly. Compared to the San Diego, Ventura, and Santa Ana Freeways in Los Angeles, or any of the access roads in London, England, New York's traffic is less perturbing.

If you drive to New York with a full load of offspring or carpoolers, expenses and the stress of driving can be shared. For weekend getaways, especially if you have a family, the cost of an automobile is relatively less than trains or buses, and you can stop wherever you please.

Against

Roughly a fourth of a middle-class income can be eaten up by a private automobile. High insurance rates, fender benders not covered by the deductible, parking, bridge and tunnel tolls, gas and maintenance are the main expenses.

The social-environmental costs of a private automobile should also be considered. With all the health foods, exercise facilities, and diet advice available in the United States, many people who are not genetically prone to obesity end up overweight because they carry out daily errands using their cars instead of their feet. These short automobile errands are especially damaging to the atmosphere because the most polluted engine exhaust is emitted during the starting and stopping of a vehicle. And beware, the daily "road warrior" routine can take its toll on the driver. For nonaggressive drivers, dodging Manhattan taxis and endless searching for parking spaces can be stressful enough to convert mellow type-B personalities into hypertensive type-As.

TRIGG.

New York is generally a pedestrian-friendly city, whose vibrant street life is best enjoyed on foot. The city's public transportation system is amazingly efficient, given that it covers such a vast area. As for excursions outside of New York, comfortable Amtrak trains lead to many interesting getaways. And even if you want or need to drive on your vacation, what you've saved by not owning a car provides a vast reserve for renting one.

In New York (unlike other U.S. cities), you won't be a social outcast if you choose not to drive. Laermer writes that the real New Yorker "may never get a driver's license (and won't miss it)."

The Verdict

The ultimate decision depends on your lifestyle. I have done it both ways in New York, with a car and without. My personal verdict is based on the aesthetics of a great New York institution: the Happy Hour. In the late afternoon, many fine bars and restaurants offer happy hours with reduced-price drinks and/or free appetizers. It's a great way to unwind after a tough day's work. But if you're going to have to drive home, you shouldn't drink. Even one martini will slow down a driver's reaction time, and in Manhattan, reaction time is often the difference between a near miss and an accident.

Happy hours exist throughout the United States, but in New York they are a cultural institution. You maximize the enjoyment of happy hour by knowing that you don't have to drive afterwards.

TAXIS

Manhattanites who consider the outer boroughs as hillbillyland can easily afford to hop in and out of "Yellow cabs" for the relatively short distances they travel. Prices are subject to increase but expect at least $2 for the first fifth of a mile, 30 cents for each additional fifth of a mile, another 30 cents per each minute-and-a-half waiting time, and a minimum surcharge between 8:00 p.m. and 6:00 a.m., with no extra charge for luggage. The rates are fixed and published, so you won't be "taken for a ride." Some tips:

- If you've got no luggage and are in a hurry to get somewhere during workday hours, it's faster to walk (crosstown) or jump into a subway (up or downtown) than to take a cab.
- If traveling to the airport from a suburb or an outer reach of a borough, it will be less expensive to hire a fixed-rate "car service" (see the phone directory Yellow Pages). You tell them your point of departure and point of arrival and they'll let you know exactly what the price is. I interviewed a car service driver, who told me that his company often takes people to other eastern cities. If several people hire a car and share the expense, it may be less expensive than flying, with no airport waiting and convenient door-to-door service.

AIRPORTS

Here's a multiple choice question for a New York geography exam. Which airport is the most convenient for people whose final destination is Manhattan?

- (a) La Guardia Airport (Queens)
- (b) John F. Kennedy International Airport (Queens)
- (c) Newark International Airport (New Jersey)

Trick Question?

I would have answered La Guardia, since it's much closer on the map to Manhattan than JFK, and since New Jersey is another state. But the answer is Newark. The trip from Newark to midtown Manhattan, comparing taxi fares or special airport buses containing luggage holds, is faster and considerably less expensive. The Olympia shuttle bus service (Newark to Manhattan) charges $10.

If you travel with only a carry-on piece of luggage, public transportation is available from both La Guardia and JFK airports, with La Guardia's short-bus plus subway or the fast M60 bus to upper Manhattan as faster alternatives than anything you can get from JFK.

A more romantic alternative is the **Delta Water Shuttle** from La Guardia to East 34th Street (25 minutes) and to Pier 11 off Wall Street (40 minutes) for somewhat less than the cost of a taxi.

The strategic location of New York's airports makes them easier to reach than airports in many other major cities in the United States (with one convenient exception being Washington National Airport).

TRAVELING OUT OF NEW YORK

Upstate New York, including the Catskill and Adirondack Mountains, rural Pennsylvania, the coast of New England (with some virtually unknown funky surfing towns in Rhode Island), and handsomely preserved Vermont villages are some of the nearby places that have managed to conserve original colonial and Victorian architecture and prevent landscapes from being overrun by suburban sprawl. Most people believe that the great West of the United States is the least inhabited and most virgin territory in the nation. Guess again. Satellite photos confirm that the Adirondack Mountain region wins this contest.

The historic city of Philadelphia, Pennsylvania lies south of New York, within a 2 to 3 hour drive; continue south for a few more hours and you reach Washington, D.C. Farther north of New York is the forgotten state of Maine, where the clock is turned back a few decades, and the culturally-engaging, Canadian province of Quebec, with its distinctive cities, Montreal and Quebec. In other words, one could remain in the northeast quadrant of the United States and find vacations to satisfy every taste.

The drive down to Philadelphia and Washington, D.C. is a dull one, unless you're aesthetically sensitive enough to perceive abstract art in the smokestacks and oil drums of New Jersey's

77

"cancer alley." Another option is catching an Amtrak train from Penn Station—a ride which is actually faster than flying to these nearby cities if airport-waiting time is factored in.

Penn Station is also the departure point for some locations to the north, via Amtrak. The north route along the Hudson River is stunningly beautiful. Renting a car (see Yellow Pages for car rental companies) is a superior alternative, as is driving your own car, if several people are traveling and you like to explore secondary roads. Travelers with a frequent flyer card can get extra miles with certain rent-a-car companies.

The **New York Port Authority Bus Terminal** on 42nd Street is no longer the seedy place it used to be, and Greyhound buses (along with Greyhound-affiliated bus companies) offer the best rates. Buses reach smaller cities and towns that trains do not. A useful tip: when traveling by Amtrak or Greyhound, ALWAYS ask about current promotions. Greyhound sometimes has specials in which a companion rides for free. Both Amtrak and Greyhound usually have single fares in which a person can make unlimited trips within a specific period of time. Train lovers will relish the thought. During one stay in New York, I was able to make round trips to Buffalo (western New York State), Washington, D.C., and Albany (capital of New York State)—all for one fare.

I've reserved my favorite getaway for last. The **Long Path**, beginning with a spectacular crossing of the George Washington Bridge can theoretically take you all the way past Albany with footpaths. Just turn right (north) after crossing the bridge, and you'll be walking above the New Jersey Palisades, with views to the right of the Hudson River. (Contour maps available in bookstores.)

Purist hikers may be disappointed when the path is occasionally overrun by suburban expansion and one has to do some road hiking. But hey, how many U.S. cities can you walk out of and be in the country within the half hour it takes to cross a bridge?

WALKING

Should you be fortunate to live in one of New York's many self-sustaining neighborhoods, walking may be the best way to get around, and it's good for your health. A Greenwich Village resident, for example, could lead a rich life without ever needing to travel on anything but his or her own two feet. Within walking distance are groceries, medical clinics, universities, art museums, bookstores, athletic facilities, flea markets, and a dazzling array of first-class restaurants and music clubs, with contiguous neighborhoods like Chinatown, Little Italy, and the East Village offering a change of pace. Needless to say, finding an apartment in such an ideal neighborhood is no easy feat.

Getting around and out of New York is relatively easy. Staying in one place is what's difficult. How to find a place to stay, whether permanent or temporary, is the subject of the next chapter.

Just how hard is it to find an apartment and then afford what you find? Yes, it's true that a large part of New York's sub-culture of the homeless have alcohol or psychological problems, often accompanied by low or absent self-esteem. But some New Yorkers, like popular tour guide Timothy Levitch make ends meet by what he calls "couch surfing," or sleeping in a network of friends' apartments and leaving part of his wardrobe in each place where he stays. By the time you read these pages, Mr. Levitch will probably have his own apartment, thanks to a filmmaker who was captivated by Levitch's "rare art of voluntary homelessness" and made a movie about him called *The Cruise*.

My non–avant garde belief is that other arts are more satisfying than voluntary or involuntary homelessness. The next chapter highly recommends an earnest search for the most suitable housing.

CHAPTER FOUR

FINDING A PLACE TO LIVE

A city housing survey showed an increase in the average share of personal income needed for rent. The figure rose from 30.8% in 1993 to 32.3% today.

—Harvey Robins, in *Social Policy*

Getting around in New York is much easier than staying put. Foreign student advisors interviewed by this writer were unanimous in concluding that finding housing (along with meeting New Yorkers) is the most challenging obstacle to surviving and thriving in New York.

The first step is to find affordable temporary lodging, a base from which one can venture out in search of more permanent housing. The best "method" for temporary lodging is to have a friend who can put you up; but even one's best friends in New York may not have space in their cramped Manhattan apartments, where some aunt or nephew is probably already sleeping on the sofa. The second step is finding long-term housing, most likely an apartment, although other options exist. And a possible third step—bypassed by a majority of New Yorkers who prefer apartment life—is to purchase a home.

Let's walk through these three stages. Wealthy readers with an unlimited bankroll can skip this chapter entirely, arrive in New York, and choose from a gourmet menu of available apartments or condominiums. But for anyone else, housing is New York's toughest hurdle. You don't have to be poor to have trouble finding a place to stay in New York.

HOTELS AND SHORT-STAY ALTERNATIVES

Hotels that advertise themselves as cheap may cost well over $100 per night. That's fine for a night or two, but what if it takes you three or four weeks to secure long-term housing? Such "bargain" hotels are easy finds in the Yellow Pages or on the Internet and don't need listing here.

Also overrated are the so-called "hotel discounters," who offer nothing of better value than the standard hotels you can find yourself, like the **Hotel Edison** (tel: 212-840-5000), in the theater district, which charges slightly above $100.

The intent of this section is to give the reader an array of alternatives. Places mentioned here, along with phone listings, are not intended as a directory. The reader can pick up a copy of *The New York Times, The Village Voice,* or any community newspaper and immediately uncover what's available (or simply browse on the Internet before arrival). Our objective is to present a conceptual array of short-term housing options with a few selected examples usually overlooked by guidebooks.

Hotels in the Boroughs

There are few hotels in the boroughs outside of Manhattan, but occasionally you can come across a spartan but clean bargain, like the **Skyway Motel**, near La Guardia Airport, in a multicultural, middle-class neighborhood in Queens, for about $70. The rooms are grim but not grimy, the bathrooms are clean, and the TV works. Besides, you're going to be out of your room searching for more long-term housing. When you get back after a discouraging first day of apartment hunting, there's consolation at the Skyway's attached bar, a multiracial neighborhood hangout with real New Yorkers instead of the typical hotel bar filled with outsiders.

The *Village Voice* (referred to as "The Voice") is distributed free on Wednesday mornings throughout the city and lists a few short-term hotel bargains within Manhattan (usually in Greenwich Village), whose weekly rates are less than the daily rates of standard Manhattan hotels. One such spot to dump your suitcase is **Hotel Riverview** (tel: 212-929-0060). Other Village hotels, like the **Pioneer Hotel** in SoHo (tel: 212-226-3525) offer daily rates that beat the Midtown hotels. Another bargain hotel that's not ideal for vacationers but serves a practical purpose for newcomers needing a temporary base is the **Herald Square Hotel** on 31st Street (tel: 212-279-4017); rooms go for well under $100 per night, and the location is not far from Koreatown.

Bed-and-Breakfasts

When B&B spots first emerged in New York, there were bargains to be had, but today, these more friendly alternatives to hotels are now part of the mainstream tourist network. A different bed-and-breakfast is Gisele Allard's **New York Bed and**

Breakfast (tel: 212-666-0559), which allows you the opportunity to stay in Harlem for bargain rates. **Bed and Breakfast Network** (tel: 212-645-8134) has a comprehensive array of B&B options, many below $100 for singles.

YMCAs and Other Residences

The city's network of **YMCAs** represents yet another alternative, and some of them have fitness centers for a fraction of what you'd pay at a chain hotel. One strategically-located YMCA is the **McBurney YMCA** on 24th Street at 7th Avenue in Chelsea, with a double room for considerably less than $100. A good workout in their gym before the day's apartment hunting can lift your spirits.

Residential hotels, among which the **Hotel Olcott** (tel: 212-877-4200) gets positive reports, offer Midtown rooms for weekly rental rates. Much more economical are the so-called "residences." The **92nd Street YW-YMCA**, at 1395 Lexington Avenue, New York, NY 10128, is a best bet, with bargain rates improving the longer you stay, but you'd better write or call in advance

(tel: 212-415-5650). The **Brandon Residence for Women**, at 340 West 85th Street (across the park from the 92nd Street YMCA), also requires advance acceptance, and you'll have to show you're a student or have a regular job. Residences have shared baths and sometimes serve meals as part of the deal, but also have minimum-stay requirements. A valuable but inexpensive purchase is *A Temporary Place to Live*, from the **Open Housing Center** (tel: 212-941-6101) at 594 Broadway, Suite 608, New York, NY 10012.

Jazz on the Park Hostel is a half-block from a secluded part of Central Park.

Hostels
Hostels are yet another alternative, and you do not have to be a youth to stay in one, nor are there minimum stay requirements. I only found one hostel, the Banana Bungalow, that practiced age discrimination. My favorite hostel, for its location and friendly atmosphere, is **Jazz on the Park Hostel** (tel: 212-932-1600) on

36 West 106th Street, a few steps away from a woodsy, secluded part of Central Park (so far undiscovered by tourists), where local residents jog, walk their dogs, and picnic. For between $25 and $35 (for a room containing between two and twelve bunks), you get a bunk bed and a basic but nourishing breakfast in a bright and friendly dining area. Common bathrooms are large enough so that clean showers and toilets are always available when necessity calls.

The grand-daddy of all hostels is **Hosteling International** (tel: 212-932-2300), also on the Upper West Side. Service is not as obviously friendly as that of Jazz on the Park, but the system works well, and many auxiliary services provided by volunteers are available. These and other hostels are conveniently located near subway stops.

University Dormitories

Yet another option for a temporary stay (summer only) are university dormitories. Among the best are **New York University** in Greenwich Village (212-998-4621), and a trio of university housing locations on the Upper West Side: **Barnard College** (tel: 212-854-8021), **Columbia University's Intern Housing** (tel: 212-854-2946), and the **International House** (tel: 212-316-8400), which also serves Columbia University students. These schools offer bargain weekly or monthly rates when students usually occupying the dorms are gone for summer vacation. This is the season when the New York Philharmonic performs free concerts and you can see Shakespeare in the Park. The package of an inexpensive dorm and New York's free summer entertainment (see Chapter 9) is unbeatable for the visiter on a tight budget.

Many of these alternatives to hotels are found in neighborhoods like the Upper West Side or Greenwich Village, which, for this writer, are more interesting when it comes to daily life than corporate and touristy Midtown.

Asking Around

Once you've found a place to dump your luggage, a more precarious but potentially serendipitous method of searching for temporary housing (while getting to know the city at the same time) is to take to the sidewalks and ask about rooms for rent within private homes or small buildings. For me this strategy works best in ethnic neighborhoods, where the informal or underground economy prevails.

By asking around in owner-run small businesses, you get to know the city from the bottom up. Grocery stores are an ideal target for this hit-and-miss search since grocers know their neighbors and often post free ads from regular customers.

The Dominicans (from Santo Domingo) in the Washington Heights neighborhood along upper Broadway are a good starting place, especially if you know Spanish. I found rooms there for anywhere from $60 to $125 (per week!). **Paulino Service** (tel: 212-740-3807) on 3868 Broadway is but one example of an ethnic realty business that specializes in rooms. Pick your favorite ethnic neighborhood for this strategy. Another possibility is the Arthur Avenue community in the Bronx, an Italian neighborhood with the old-country feel.

The smart traveler who wishes to interact with the people of New York City encounters intriguing alternatives beyond the mainstream hotel scene. None of these alternatives will be as comfortable as the Crowne Plaza Hotel or the Sheraton Park Avenue (for only $350 per night), but all of them will bring you closer to the true rhythm of the city.

APARTMENTS

The "American Dream" is based on owning your own home. Either New Yorkers have *chosen* to not buy into the American Dream, or the structure of their crowded city has not allowed them to. A comparison of the 20 largest cities in the United States shows that New York has the smallest proportion of its population living in owner-occupied dwellings (houses, condominiums, or co-ops); only 28 percent of New Yorkers live in owner-occupied residences. Compare this to other major cities: Houston, 74.4 percent; Philadelphia, 61.9 percent; Charlotte, 55 percent; Detroit, 52.9 percent; Denver, 49.2 percent; Seattle, 48.9 percent; San Diego, 48.3 percent; Dallas, 44.1 percent; Los Angeles, 39.4 percent; San Francisco, 34.5 percent; Miami, 33.1 percent.

A large number of New Yorkers who succumbed to the dream have fled to the suburbs. Many of them originally intended to participate in city life, but the long distance commute got the best of them. Other suburbanites yearn to return to the city, but they are paralyzed from doing so for they know they would have to sacrifice a big chunk of the living space now filled with accumulated material possessions they cannot part with. Those who have remained within the five boroughs and nearby extensions of the city, such as Hoboken, New Jersey (only 21.6 percent of whose residents live in owner-occupied dwellings), can be seen as subversives or anti-patriots for rejecting the icon of the single-family dwelling with the two-car garage.

Newcomers to New York who wish to fit in with this rent-paying culture must search for an apartment. You can do this by reading the classified ads and making phone calls, visiting a broker and having him or her take you around, or simply asking around. Using the one-bedroom dwelling as a yardstick for comparison, apartments in reasonably safe neighborhoods in Manhattan can run from $1,200 up to over $2,500 per month (on the Upper East Side) or more. The boroughs represent a fair alternative, but if you want to be closest to Manhattan, you'll pay; in Brooklyn Heights, one-bedroom apartments go for above $1,000 per month. In rapidly gentrifying Hoboken, rents are only about 10 percent less than in Manhattan.

Typical Manhattan apartment facade.

Outside of Manhattan

The formula is simple but has its exceptions: the farther away you are from Manhattan, especially in communities where one must take the bus to get to the subway, the lower the rent. In Queens, within walking distance of a subway line, one can find one-bedroom units between $600 (in block-like highrises like Lefrak City) and $850 (in Jamaica Estates). In Brooklyn or the Bronx, one comes across comparable one-bedroom apartments for as cheap as the high-$500s to as much as the $800s in the woodsy areas near the big parks.

Much has been written about rent-control apartments and other rent-stabilization variations, but these cheap dwellings are almost impossible to find. Most rent-controlled or rent-stabilized apartments never reach the market. More flexible laws on sublets may enable you to find a dweller in one of these affordable apartments who has a year work contract abroad and wishes to find a subletter. But short of stalking tenants in rent-stabilized apartments, or wining and dining them, the newcomer will face steep odds against finding such an ideal abode. Native New Yorkers with larger networks of friends and family represent the competition.

Sublets

Increasingly, New Yorkers are willing to settle for a long-term but temporary apartment, by subletting furnished apartments for interim periods of anywhere from six months to two years. Frequent moves are the downside, but less expensive rent in interesting neighborhoods is the plus. See the "sublets" sections of classified ads, or better yet, get a jump by choosing your preferred neighborhoods and asking around. The very few brokers specializing in furnished sublets may charge either a month's rent or a 15% fee, but this may be worth it if the period of the sublet is parallel to the period of your stay in New York, considering the significant savings in furnishings and appliances. Brokers are advertised in the classifieds and Yellow Pages.

One painstaking way to avoid a broker is to check out community bulletin boards in supermarkets, university student unions, laundromats, and even in large apartment buildings themselves.

Follow the Artists

A craftier strategy of finding a bargain is by studying demographics. Where are the artists beginning to move? It's a New York tradition; artists zero in on a depressed neighborhood with cheap rents, move in, and renovate the area in their funky way. This process then attracts the very same commercial interests that had previously shunned the neighborhood. Eventually, upscale commerce moves in and the artist-pioneers are priced out of the neighborhood they rescued and are obligated to move to cheaper surroundings.

Talk to artists, actors, writers (not the ones in chic galleries or on the best-seller lists) and ask them where the artists are beginning to move TODAY. This way, you should be able to get four or five years of relatively inexpensive living in a dynamic scenario until you get priced out. Or, perhaps by then you can afford to stay. When attempting to forecast the up-and-coming neighborhood, do not rely on sources based on conventional wisdom. When a run-down neighborhood gets too much publicity too early, become suspicious.

The Informal Economy

Another strategy, similar to the one applied in the search for temporary housing, is to choose an ethnic neighborhood. Even in Manhattan, there are various areas dominated by less-than-upscale ethnic groups where less expensive apartments are available. Some ethnic neighborhoods are as safe or safer than others with a good reputation. The Upper West Side of Manhattan, heavily populated with folks from Santo Domingo, is probably an area with a future, for example, although that future may have come already and rents may have skyrocketed by the time you read this book. But the concept remains valid.

Sharing

This is a touchy subject, for even the best of friends may find they are incompatible when sharing the same living quarters, as in the classic film, *The Odd Couple*. On the other hand, when it comes to occupying the same space, strangers may be more compatible. A striking testimony of the scarce housing market is the fact that New Yorkers, perhaps the most individualistic of all U.S. citizens (and thus the least likely to tolerate each other), have adopted sharing as a major housing alternative.

But if you're a newcomer unaccustomed to New Yorkers, how do you know that the apartment you've agreed to share does not have among its residents tomorrow's version of The Mad Bomber, Son of Sam, or the World Trade Center terrorists?

91

Both the *New York Times* classifieds ("Apartments to Share") and the *Voice* ("Shares") offer ample opportunities to find an attractive place for less. New York's largest roommate agency is **Transworld Roommate Service** (tel: 212-243-6999; website address is *http://www.transworldroommates.com*). In the annals of commercial guarantees, Transworld offers one of the weirdest: "Transworld will guarantee your compatibility for 120 days." How did they choose 120, rather than 90 or 180? Perhaps psychology research has documented that the 121st day of a sharing arrangement is the straw that breaks the camel's back when it comes to the weight of human relations.

Other share agencies are advertised in the classifieds. Even if you choose to bypass the agency route, you have the opportunity of interviewing the sharing person who wants you to give him or her half the rent—before you accept any deal.

Financial Arrangements

Once you've found an apartment, be prepared to lay down a deposit (usually equivalent to a month's rent) while they do a credit search. Make sure you've got money in the bank, or a steady job, or have a perfect credit rating, or all of the above. Letters of reference might help as well, since this is a sellers' market. A standard measure for landlords is to expect the rent you promise to pay is no more than 25 percent of your income. But a city housing survey published on February 19, 1997 showed that the average share of personal income needed by New Yorkers for rent had risen to 32.3%.

Once your deposit has been accepted as the first month's rent, you'll be asked for a security deposit, which, in the best-case-scenario, will be deposited in an interest-earning account and will be refunded with interest at the end of your lease.

An apartment lease is not as exciting as a supermarket tabloid, but scrutinize the lease carefully.

92

Discrimination

Laws in New York prohibit discrimination based on ethnic background, race, or sexual orientation; landlords are also prohibited from rejecting potential tenants because they have children. But what appears on paper does not necessarily match reality.

New York is believed by many to be the nation's most liberal and tolerant city, but ask most people of color if they were treated fairly by landlords in neighborhoods where their non-white ethnic group was not in the majority. If you are a person of color who also has children, double the projected obstacles. And after you move in, the struggle may not be over. In 1995, for example, a Hispanic family that had just moved into a neighborhood in Queens received a housewarming present of a dead rabbit tied to their door.

Back in late 1995, Peter Feuerherd, assistant editor of the *Long Island Catholic*, wrote that "political leaders in this city, both white and black, see segregated neighborhoods as a kind of natural selection which shall remain undisturbed, an arrangement with which elites in both communities have grown comfortable."

Evidence of the extent of discrimination by landlords is primarily anecdotal. From this writer's experience, New York, even with its history of hate crimes, is a much less segregated city than Chicago or the Washington, D.C. metropolitan area.

Housing Concerns for Parents: The School Strategy

As a parent, my favorite strategy is to choose a neighborhood by the quality of the school where my child or adolescent will be going. I've done this in cities like Los Angeles and Chicago with no more help than word of mouth. In those cities, I was willing to pay a little extra for housing, which was more than compensated for by the peace of mind that comes when you know your kids are in a good school.

New York City makes this task easier by releasing report cards on all its schools. Before obtaining report cards from the

93

Board of Education (tel: 718-935-3555) or the **Public Education Association** (tel: 212-868-1640), understand that report cards judging schools may be incomplete or simplistic, since the criteria do not take into consideration things like overcrowding or number of students who switched schools during the year.

In other words, it may not be fair to use report cards for blanket condemnation of teachers or school administrations; but these ratings remain a useful tool for the parent, who does not care whose fault it is that a school is failing so long as his or her kids are not in that school. In general, but with notable exceptions, the income-level of the neighborhood correlates with the success of the school—the higher the income, the superior the students' test scores and graduation rates.

However, the now decentralized New York school system is open to competition, with magnet schools, open-zoned and open-enrollment schools, and alternative schools with their own programs. With such competition, the income-scholastic success correlation often fails. For example, 76.7 percent of the students in New York's 1997 top-rated elementary school, Public School 223 Mott Hall in Manhattan, were classified as poor enough to be eligible for a free school lunch. The same school at the Intermediate School (I.S.) level had 80 percent of its students qualifying for free lunch and yet came in second place in city-wide reading scores.

"Surprisingly," writes Clara Hemphill in her *The Parents' Guide to New York's Best Elementary Schools* (SOHO Press, 1997), "some of the best schools are in poor and working-class neighborhoods." Not only do the very best public schools in New York compete with the best private schools, but if parents are willing to enroll their children in a school with a high percentage of ethnic or minority students, they have a better chance of getting a unique educational program. There are some schools in Queens where 40 languages are spoken within the student population! The ethnic composition of New York public schools is roughly 35 percent Hispanic, 35 percent third black, about 15 percent white, and 10 percent Asian.

It is fair to say that people who understand New York's schools are well on their way to having a far better understanding of New York than urbanologists who have never visited a classroom. I grew up in New York City schools and am well aware that some can be very tough on children while others are mellow. One simple method for re-evaluating a potential school in a potential neighborhood of choice is to watch the kids as they leave school and chat with the school guard.

I have included a brief section on schools at this juncture because in New York, when parents must evaluate and choose a neighborhood, the school factor should come first. Don't be like one couple I know who chose the wrong neighborhood and ended up with a son who carried the emotional scars from his New York school days all the way to adulthood.

Whether you are a parent or not, remember that housing in New York is not a right but a privilege, and finding the right roof requires privileged research and knocking on a lot of doors. Even at the height of New York's economic renaissance (during the tenure of Mayor Rudy Giuliani), the number of soup kitchens feeding the homeless went up from 681 in 1994 to 740 in 1995 to 903 in 1996, suggesting that an increasing number of New Yorkers cannot afford basic necessities — or that New York has suddenly become a much more charitable city.

Between 1994 and 1997, rents rose 18%, and even "stabilized" rental units were increasing between 5% and 7% over that period. Between 1993 and 1997, during a period of non-inflation in most sectors, the number of city apartments renting for less that $600 declined by 152,000, approximately 14%.

But before you become alarmed by these statistics, consider that for comparable neighborhoods, rent remains lower in New York than it would be in Paris or London.

BUYING A HOME

When considering the final housing alternative, home ownership, there are several common recommendations for New York. First, the newcomer should spend a basic acquaintance period in the metropolitan area before buying anything. Weekend scouting excursions to the different boroughs and suburbs would seem to be a prerequisite to avoid what happened to a friend:

"We bought the house after we'd gotten familiar with the east side of the neighborhood, and it looked great. But after we saw the west side," he lamented, "we knew we'd made a mistake."

Without knowing the market, a house that is truly a bargain might seem expensive compared to what you're used to in Springfield, Illinois or London, Ontario. Conversely, an overpriced piece of property with no future might seem like a bargain if you're comparing it to a comparable unit in Springfield, Virginia or London, England.

A second recommendation concerns the time you expect to remain in New York. Property values definitely rise in the long run, but if you are in it for the short run, you could lose money, and renting would make more financial sense. During the first few years when you "own" a house or condominium you'll face your highest expenses: a greater proportion of mortgage payments going to interest, the closing costs (which include attorney's fees, points, title insurance, inspections, various purchasing taxes and fees, escrow charges), and the amount of time invested that will take you away from the original purpose of your stay.

Long-term benefits of home ownership include an expected rise in real estate values (if you've chosen the right location), various tax deductions, and the knowledge that some of what you are paying is going to equity, which would not be the case if you were renting.

Purchasing a house or a condominium is an extremely complex process, best left in the hands of a real estate broker, with the ultimate intervention of a lawyer. Co-ops present an even touchier situation, since you don't know where your property ends and your neighbor's begins, and in order to sell, your buyer must be approved by the other shareholders in the co-op. In both co-ops and condominiums, you are not the owner of the land beneath you, and maintenance of common property requires monthly assessment charges which do not go into equity and might rise alarmingly every year.

The best way to find a sincere and aggressive broker is by word of mouth. As soon as you get to know home or condominium owners, ask them about the real estate expert who brokered their purchase. Before you begin your search, make sure you've got plenty of evidence in your behalf for your credit rating, and be prepared for a required down payment of 20 percent. Lenders will expect you to be able to handle a purchase price of no more than three or four times your yearly income.

As with apartment hunting, in the realm of real estate, it's best to find an up-and-coming neighborhood.

Few newcomers to New York will be going directly from the arrival gate of the airport to a real estate broker, and most will eventually opt for renting, as most New Yorkers do, so there's no point in belaboring the subject of real estate purchasing in a book like this. Just remember how the Japanese took heavy losses after their unfettered investments in New York real estate in the 1980s.

Housing is New York's greatest obstacle, and statistics on cost and availability are not promising. But after having had the chance to search for housing in both Paris and New York, New York emerges as the easier of the two. And in New York (as in Paris), a fair chunk of your rent expenses are compensated for by the efficient and inexpensive public transportation systems, both within the city and extending beyond.

CHAPTER FIVE

EATING IN NEW YORK:
Culinary Promiscuity

One of the best kept secrets in New York is an Italian restaurant, run by a mother and son, out of the way on First Avenue between 61st and 62nd.

—Art K., a New York restaurant connoisseur

Do you live to eat or eat to live? New York has alternatives for both philosophies. Tempted by the world's greatest variety of foods, eat-to-live advocates may succumb a live-to-eat way of life. To assuage the guilt of gluttony, New Yorkers can run off the excess fat and calories over many miles of attractive wooded paths in the city's lush parks.

MARKETS AND GROCERIES

For those on a strict budget, multipurpose supermarkets offer the best value and the most practical way to shop for food. But it's more fun to frequent specialty food venues, fish mongers, outdoor produce stands, greengrocers, and farmers' markets. Shopping in stages can be time consuming, but in New York, the aesthetic rewards may make it worth your while.

Many New Yorkers who live to eat will drive or bus to their favorite ethnic neighborhood in pursuit of the goodies and personal service that you just can't get at the supermarket around the corner. In order to compete, many supermarkets have their own specialty bakeries and delis within.

Those who hate shopping for food in any of its forms should try one of New York's increasing number of **farmers' markets**. At these festive outdoor venues (sponsored by the Council of the Environment of New York City), farmers and bakers from New

An Italian butcher at Arthur Avenue in the Bronx.

Produce market in Brighton Beach, a Russian neighborhood.

York State, New Jersey, and Connecticut truck in their produce. Aside from the normal meats and produce, some of these markets sell wines, honey, and flowers. Prices are reasonable and the produce is fresher than what you'd find in a supermarket. One of the original models for these outdoor shopping experiences is the **Union Square greenmarket**, which is held your-round on Mondays, Wednesdays, Fridays, and Saturdays at 17th Street and Broadway in Manhattan. Another year-round farmers' market is held at Brooklyn's Borough Hall on Tuesdays and Saturdays.

In general, expect these setups to last from 8:00 a.m. to 6:00 p.m. Most greenmarkets are confined to spring, summer, and autumn months, and take a vacation during the cold winter months when New Yorkers are more likely to prefer the warmth of an indoor supermarket. To locate the outdoor farmers' market nearest your neighborhood, call the **Council on the Environment of New York City** at 212-477-3220.

RESTAURANTS

The average per-person spending on a meal at a New York restaurant is $31.68. If you thought New York was expensive, you were right. The average restaurant visit in the United States costs $21.67, or 32 percent less than one in New York. But eating out in New York may be at least 32 percent more satisfying compared to most other parts of the United States. (San Francisco and New Orleans residents deserve the right to disagree.)

Consider too that the average cost per meal in Paris is $50.81, while London does not lag far behind at $45.58. In fact, these averages are for comparable upscale restaurants. New York, more so than either London or Paris, offers a wide array of moderately-priced dining alternatives (although in London you can eat fabulously well for less at Indian restaurants, and in Paris, you find attractive *prix fixe* lunchtime bargains).

But New York outdoes Europe; here, the whole world's cuisines are attending a permanent international food festival. Restaurants come and go, but as many prospering New Yorkers at the turn of the century are choosing to eat out more often, new restaurants emerge in unlikely corners of the city. If the boom

THE THREE WISE DINERS

101

should turn to bust, many of the restaurants now thriving might disappear overnight.

Given the volatile restaurant scenario, the newcomer is advised to read the extensive narrative restaurant reviews in *The Village Voice* or *The New York Press*. No book on New York can outdo these superb up-to-date sources.

Here are a few Manhattan restaurants that are consensus favorites among live-to-eat New Yorkers interviewed for this book (see Yellow Pages for addresses and phone numbers).

- **Pietro's** reputedly has the best steak in town (but I ordered pasta there). Others argue that **Peter Luger's** and **Spark's** serve steak of equal quality.

- The expensive **Primavera** is one Upper East Side spot where newcomers are especially welcome; try the baby goat house special. In the same league is **Le Cirque**, with its carnival decor and its owner mingling with the guests to see if everything is alright. Now that Le Cirque's chef Daniel Boulud has left to form his own restaurant (**Cafe Boulud**), how long will Le Cirque maintain its status? For other French delicacies like the sea food soup bouillabaisse, try **Le Jardin Bistro**.

- Some New Yorkers swear by **I Trulli** (which offers several dishes that highlight asparagus) as one of the city's best eclectic restaurants. The East Village's **Miracle Grill** makes Tex-Mex food into a gourmet experience for a reasonable price, but Southwesterners might not recognize that this stuff comes from their part of the country. The moderately-priced **Mi Concha** in the West Village passes my two-part test for Mexican restaurants: (1) it has *mole*, an ancient Aztec dish which includes sesame, chocolate, and two different types of dark, hot peppers as part of an 18-ingredient sauce served over chicken and rice; and (2) its guacamole is chunky—not like the blender guacamole in many Mexican restaurants that should be bottled as baby food.

- Some of the city's best restaurants specialize in Italian food. **Po** is run by the famous TV chef Mario Batali, with creative Italian country cooking.
- The top two Jewish delis are reputed to be **Carnegie Deli** and the **Second Avenue Deli**.
- Seek out Harlem for soul food, with **Sylvia's Kitchen** among the neighborhood's leading restaurants.
- Vegetarians have an ample choice of restaurants, with one of New Yorkers' favorites found in Soho: **Souen**, which boasts a Japanese, macrobiotic persuasion. But many good non-vegetarian restaurants have their superb vegetarian dishes, including the Village spot called **Salaam Bombay**.
- The East Village, the West Village, Midtown, and the Upper East Side are restaurant havens, but some of New York's best kept culinary secrets are found off the beaten path, such as **Via Oreto**, an Italian restaurant run by a mother and son all the way east on First Avenue between 61st and 62nd Street.

Targeting a Neighborhood . . . And Other Strategies

An alternative strategy in restaurant hunting is to land in an ethnic neighborhood in one of the boroughs, where you know the food will be authentic. Try Astoria in Queens for Greek food, Arthur Avenue in the Bronx for Italian food, and Brooklyn's Atlantic Avenue for Arabic food. Back in Manhattan you can't go wrong with an all-Chinese menu in Chinatown, and perhaps New York's most up-and-coming ethnic food is Korean, on West 32nd Street (Koreatown). Try **Kang Suh**, but don't fill up on the savory free appetizers (pickled vegetables and other spicy goodies) or you won't have room for the main round.

In a macro-restaurant scenario, one micro-strategy would be to pick out two or three good restaurants, become a regular, and receive preferential treatment. Another strategy would be to choose a place with live music, such as live salsa atmosphere of

Bayamo on Broadway. Skip the usual restaurant-then-entertainment process. Why not get all in one?

My apologies to the Thais, the Malaysians, the Ukrainians, and 88 other ethnic groups whose restaurants were not mentioned here. We've skipped an encyclopedic list of restaurants, presenting instead several practical yet creative strategies for those who eat out as entertainment. If eating out is a necessity rather than a luxury, you may prefer some of the budget alternatives that follow.

Buffets

New York City offers a profusion of ethnic buffet restaurants — *sans* famous chefs — but with quaint or bizarre atmospheres. When one is eating out for practical reasons for no special occasion, these places offer great value. Two examples:

- Pakistani and Indian food at **Shaheen** (99 Lexington Avenue, at 27th Street), where you can find a $5.95 all-you-can-eat lunch buffet between 11:00 a.m. and 4:00 p.m. and an $8.95 dinner buffet — vegetarian or non-vegetarian.
- **Caliente Cab Company**, a block from Washington Square, goes one better with a $4.95 all-you-can-eat lunch buffet, with Mexican and non-Mexican specialties. This is not gourmet Mexican food, but the beans are good, and the price includes a healthy salad bar and dessert.

Pay by Weight

In Midtown, there are other types of buffets with exhaustive choices of food (usually operated by Asians). You choose the goodies, take your plate to the cashier, and the cashier charges you by the weight of your food. What you see is what you get. Don't expect any atmosphere in these delis, but they represent a practical, more tasty, and potentially more nutritious (depending on what you choose) alternative to a fast food restaurant. If you spend $10 at one of these places then you have a serious overeating problem.

FAST FOOD

New York has all the same fast food chains whose tentacles have spread to every corner of the world, plus a few local chains as well. McDonald's, Burger King, and KFC have little to do with life in New York, and it is recognized that the fast "foods" in these places are marketed for their recreational value, especially for kids. The nutritional value of such foods is questionable at best—they are sky-high in sodium, and overwhelming in their fat content.

Strategically, a fast food place may come in handy if you have to use the bathroom, if it's raining outside and you need a place to dry off, or if you're tired and wish to sit around over a cup of coffee, anonymously, without anyone bothering you. If you carry a diary and need a place to sit down and make important entries while they're fresh in your mind, a fast food place gives you table space and privacy. Some fast food places have game rooms for young children, so they may become a convenient stop-off in a moment of parental stress. Generally, fast food places have a function, but it has little to do with food.

STREET FOOD

New York street food, on the other hand, is usually served fast and does have its appeal. No place in the world has better pizza stands. In a long-forgotten Jimmy Breslin movie, a recently-arrived Italian immigrant is taken by his New York family to have pizza, and he remarks: "Hey, this New York food is delicious!"

Other New York street food traditions include Nathan's hot dogs (with mustard and sauerkraut), Jewish knishes (a type of spicy potato pie), Chinese egg rolls, Middle Eastern falafel and couscous (at Natural Foods), Greek gyros, and a wide variety of Danish pastries. This is just the beginning. Each ethnic group has its own specialty. Let's not forget the ubiquitous pretzel stands, whose scenic function makes up for their minimal impact on taste buds. (My son tried a pretzel and never asked for one again.)

Is New York street food more nutritious than corporate fast food? Probably not much, but if you choose carefully, you will be rewarded. A Hebrew National Deli Frankfurter (2.3 ounces), typical at many New York deli hot dog counters, has 20 milligrams of cholesterol, compared to a smaller 1.6 oz. regular brand hot dog that has 30 mg of cholesterol. A McDonald's Filet-O-Fish has 50 mg of cholesterol, and a Big Mac wins the cholesterol contest with 103 mg. A worthy alternative would be three patties of falafel in a pita bread at a Middle Eastern food stand, with no cholesterol at all. Even the hummus sauce that goes with it has none.

Not so healthy, but considerably more tasty than a Big Mac, is a pastrami on rye sandwich at a typical Jewish delicatessen (deli), with plenty of mustard and a dill pickle—enough sodium to last a whole week. (Insiders prefer corned beef over pastrami.) Lox (smoked salmon) and bagels with cream cheese are another potent Jewish delicacy, especially tasty with a steamy cup of rich coffee.

LEAD US NOT TO TEMPTATION?

Trappist monks with spartan diets should stay clear of New York City. The culinary temptations are infinite. It's not like France, where, even with an immense variety of regional dishes, you're still faithfully eating French food at the designated hour with few between-meal snacks. In New York, it's normal to eat at all hours and even to switch cuisine on a daily basis—the equivalent of culinary promiscuity.

Chapter Six

ON THE BANKS OF MANHATTAN

(and Other Transactions)

Please remember that past performance is not indicative of future results.

—a New York stockbroker

People from other regions of the United States often perceive New York as money-driven city. It is, after all, the investment and banking capital of the United States. Yet, for the vast majority of New Yorkers, whether they have lots of it or not, money is simply a means to fulfill other needs in their lives.

By making the right money decisions upon arrival, the newcomer to New York can minimize the need to think too much about money later on.

107

BANKING

Savings and checking accounts are federally insured, so for the safety of one's deposits, there's little difference between choosing one of New York's two major banks, **Citibank** and **Chase Manhattan** (taken over by **Chemical Bank**), or one of the many smaller banks. Some of New York's "small" banks are larger than the largest banks of developing countries, so small is a relative term. The two largest banks have branches throughout the city, making them attractive for people on the run.

It pays to shop around among smaller banks (some of which include **Republic, Apple, East New York Savings,** and **Emigrant**) for the best interest rates on savings and minimum-balance checking accounts. A few phone calls will tell you which banks permit the smallest minimum balance for the account holder to be exempt from a service charge, and which ones have the lowest maintenance charges. To apply for these and other types of accounts, bring two pieces of identification containing your signature.

International travelers may prefer a bank with branches in foreign countries, but don't be fooled by the fact that many foreign banks use the same names as those in New York. Sometimes the best bank for foreign linkage is the least obvious. Consult with an international banking officer in any bank you're considering.

If you prefer the impersonal method of banking electronically through your PC, ask the bank's account officer for an explanation of their system.

Shop around for the best bank according to your personal, family, and business needs. Much of this shopping may be done by phone, provided that you can tolerate aggravating voice mail systems. ("Press '1' if you want information on our special Whitewater investment account, press '2' if you would like to purchase our memorial Richard Nixon gold coins, call back later if you wish to speak to a human being.") Such automated phone systems could lead one day to the downfall of civilization. The bank whose phone system permits the easiest access to a personal service representative may be the best for you if your life already contains banking complexities.

CREDIT

The best way to be loved by credit card companies is to owe money, and then pay it back, preferably slowly enough so your interest payments become inflated. Credit these days is international so foreigners planning to come to New York can arrive with a good credit record already established by using an international credit card.

For international travelers, **VISA** and **MasterCard** are the cards most likely to be accepted abroad. Beware of offers for low-interest credit cards that, following a period as brief as six months, raise their interest rate from 3.9 percent to 19.9 percent. Sometimes it's better to pay a yearly maintenance fee if you get something in return in the way of service or premiums. Especially valuable is a frequent-flyer credit card that gives you a mile for every dollar you spend. Buy everything on credit, pay it back on time, and the mileage adds up fast.

INSURANCE

By contributing handsomely to both major political parties, the powerful **health insurance** lobby has made sure that the United States does not adopt some of the more humane and efficient health care systems found in places like Canada and Europe. The *New England Journal of Medicine* reported in 1999 that the U.S. health care system is "the most expensive and most inadequate in the developed world," and that people in the United States pay $3,925 per person for health care each year. Second place is Switzerland, but it's not even close, with the Swiss spending $2,500 per person. The unwieldy private health insurance system in the United States, with its innumerable middlemen, is largely to blame for this incongruous situation.

If you get lucky, your employer will pay at least part of your health insurance policy, provided you accept his plan, which will more often than not be an **HMO (health maintenance organiza-tion)** with less personal attention but greater cost-effectiveness. If you work freelance, you can either "wing it" and live without insurance, as an increasing number of U.S. citizens have chosen to do, or pay stiff monthly premiums for this "protection."

Stories abound of uninsured people being denied medical care at major hospitals. In February of 1998, for example, a mother and her 1-week-old baby daughter were turned away from a routine visit at an outpatient clinic of New York Methodist Hospital in Brooklyn for lack of money or insurance. Five weeks later, the baby died of malnutrition; the mother had erroneously thought she was adequately breast-feeding the baby. Her error would have been immediately detected during the simple visit she was denied. The State Department of Health officially faulted the hospital.

Hospitals cannot turn people away from their emergency rooms, but the markup on one's bill will be outrageous. One young lady suffering from flu symptoms was taken to an emergency room by her mother. It turned out she had a heavy cold. She was treated and left the hospital in two and a half hours. The bill added up to nearly $2,000. If a non-life-threatening health problem does occur, first try for the "urgent care" clinic, whose rates will be somewhat less than the typical emergency room.

If such horror stories convince you to seek out an HMO, the highest-ranked New York HMO by *U.S. News and World Report* (October 13, 1997) was **Kaiser Foundation**. Consult any branch of the New York Public Library for the most recent HMO rankings.

Mark Weisbrot, research director of the Preamble Center (a public policy think tank), wrote that "a better idea would be to provide universal health insurance for everyone, with the government as insurer." The United States is the only country in the developed world without some form of "single-payer" health care system. As a result, the population of uninsured U.S. inhabitants is larger than the population of most countries in the world. Among these uninsured are a large contingent of people who

111

practice preventive health in their daily life, maintaining diets of based on whole grains and fruits, avoiding fats, and doing regular healthy exercise.

Health insurance involves more complicated decisions than **auto insurance**. For car owners, auto liability insurance is required by law. The same common sense strategy applies: shop around for the best deal, but also check publications like *Consumer Reports* for ratings of the companies. Auto insurance rates in New York State jumped 36 percent between 1990 and 1996, even though the number of accidents involving personal injury dropped during the same period. The jump in premiums was caused by a near doubling of personal injury suits. The best way to avoid soaring insurance rates and litigimania is to take the subway.

INVESTMENTS

Investing in the **stock market** was once the passion of a privileged elite. Since deregulated banks began paying miserly interest rates, an increasing number of common people are investing in the market, mostly through mutual funds. Most of the largest brokerage houses and mutual fund companies list New York addresses. Stock mutual fund accounts are, of course, uninsured, and it is possible to lose money from your principal. Stock market investing might not be a worthy subject for this book except for the fact that in New York you will inevitably hear conversations involving big "scores" on the market. You'll hear people say they've doubled their money overnight with an underrated company on the NASDAQ, and you'll be tempted again and again to try to make a killing.

A general principle I've found to be true in all gambling (the stock market is a form of gambling) is that the more people who think something is good, the less likely it will be good. As I write these lines, the current rising market is proving me wrong. But even the chairman of the Federal Reserve has declared that he thought stocks were overvalued.

After a day of losses, Wall Street empties out quickly, with one straggler contemplating the day's events —and a teen who couldn't care less.

Conservative investors choose **bonds**, but bond mutual funds are also uninsured, and historically, bonds have yielded inferior returns when compared to stocks, and it's not even close. The best advice for investing in the market is to first become studious and educated. The reference librarian at any branch of the New York Public Library will provide a wealth of statistical materials and updated reports, both for individual stocks and mutual funds. Especially helpful are the city's business libraries, such as the **New York Public Library: Science, Industry and Business Library** on 188 Madison Avenue (at 34th Street).

Actively-investing New Yorker friends insisted to me that the market could continue to rise even if it is overvalued, especially since many U.S. corporations are now unchallenged in the global market. However, one should be wary if peace should break out around the world, for the large "defense" industry and many collateral industries that gain profits from the defense budget

113

would be obligated to deflate. The defense industry, of course, is subsidized by the federal government, its major client. Every time there is a bombing mission (a.k.a. "peace mission"), weapons and other technologies are used, and this expensive hardware must be replaced. Few economists would disagree that the United States escaped its severe 1930s depression largely because of World War II. The Cold War maintained defense spending at a high level. Now, regional conflicts around the world help sustain defense industries.

The stock market has a historical record of a reliable increase in value, even when crashes and corrections are included, but much of the market's history is based on war and cold-war economies. What will happen in this type of economic system in a peacetime economy is less predictable in the absence of past performances.

Another question for investors: what will happen when the immense number of baby boomers begin to cash in their retirement accounts between the years 2005 and 2015? The funds from these accounts now make up a large portion of the stock market reserves. Will the market suddenly deflate?

Individual Retirement Accounts (IRAs) and other variations allow us to invest in the market with tax deductions and without having to pay taxes on profits until we withdraw our investment. Withdrawal prior to retirement involves a heavy financial penalty. By withdrawing after retirement, when one's income is lower, the profits from the retirement account will be exposed to a lower tax rate.

If you do decide to invest in a mutual fund, consider that "no-load" funds with exceptional performance records are available in place of other funds with stiff brokerage fees. Who needs the advice of a hard-sell broker (who demands a hefty commission) when you can make your own educated investment decisions and pay minimum commissions at a discount brokerage like **Charles H. Schwab**?

114

Brokerage firms and mutual fund companies routinely publish a disclaimer that their financial analyses are based on past performances which are not necessarily indicators of future performance. Investment is a form of gambling with a reasonable chance for success. It can be fun, provided it is done with a foundation of knowledge, preferably your own, and with a bankroll separate from one's family budget.

INCOME TAXES

People working anywhere in the United States must deal with the **Internal Revenue Service (IRS)**, paying federal income taxes on or before the April 15 deadline each year. Every time the government engages in "tax reform," the complexity of the tax forms increases. You may choose to calculate your own taxes, as I do, or you may hire a tax accountant or a chain tax firm like **H.R. Block**, the McDonald's of tax return service. Either way, save all receipts, since (by law) one must keep documented records of one's tax return. For free answers to your tax return questions, call the IRS at 800-829-1040, or visit the IRS office at 120 Church Street in Lower Manhattan. IRS representatives won't do your taxes, but they'll answer your questions, almost always with impeccable cordiality.

An economically feasible and legal way to reduce the impact of taxes is to make a living with one's hobby. In this way, expenses earmarked for enjoyment and recreation, if they produce income, will be tax deductible. The trip of a florist to an international flower show would be deductible, as would ski trips of one who publishes a skiing newsletter.

Free IRS booklets explain all these exotic deductions. Some of the world's best satire is found in such booklets, in those passages that spell out tax loopholes that allow the wealthiest of U.S. citizens to obtain significant tax deductions. But those loopholes were made part of the law by clever congressional lawyers,

115

not fastidious IRS bureaucrats. Foreigners have been surprised to learn that when I've unwittingly overpaid my taxes, the IRS has sent me a refund, without my asking!

"In my country," said one South American, "if I overpaid my taxes, I'd never see the money again!"

New Yorkers also pay state and city taxes on a combined form, largely based on the federal forms so as to minimize further confusion. Taxpayer assistance for this return is 800-CALLTAX. New Yorkers earning $50,000 or more in income pay higher local taxes than in any other major city in the United States. The trade-off is that New York ranked 47th in property taxes among major cities.

New York state and local taxes are among the most "progressive" in that lower incomes pay a significantly lower proportion of their income in taxes. New Yorkers earning $25,000 per year paid a lower proportion of local taxes than inhabitants with the same income level in five other major U.S. cities. If low state and local taxes were to determine your preferred city, you'd bypass New York and choose New Orleans and Los Angeles.

SHOPPING

In my family, the biggest sin was to buy retail.
—Howard Prince (played by Woody Allen) in the film *The Front*

The only other book I've seen dedicated to newcomers in New York looks like the Yellow Pages when it comes to shopping. Anyone can find department stores like **Macy's**, **Bloomingdales** or the more upscale **Saks Fifth Avenue** and **Christian Dior**, and Yellow Pages are readily available at no charge, so we won't repeat easily obtainable phone numbers here.

If you shop for fun, New York's thousands of quirky specialty stores await you. These stores are best found by strolling mainly in Manhattan, often on less glamorous avenues and sidestreets.

Bargain shoppers prefer the city's many "discount stores." To find them, just look in the Yellow Pages under the category you want (furniture, carpets, computers, etc.) and you'll see the "discount" displayed prominently in ads for this category of commerce.

Some serious shopping may be done through consultants. I hired a computer consultant to help me choose the best used computer for my needs. I was pleasantly rewarded. My computer was located through the Internet, from a reputable company with a guarantee, and I received personal guidance for using my new toy. One company that can take you through the process for a very reasonable fee is **Personal Computer Power Center** (tel: 212-315-0809) at 1650 Broadway, in Midtown Manhattan.

Window shopping at Christian Dior, Fifth Avenue.

More interesting, and combining pragmatism with recreation, are the city's alternative shopping venues, which include flea markets, neighborhoods with product-specific specialties, auctions, thrift shops, yard sales (which also may be called rummage, moving or estate sales), warehouse outlets, and sample sales.

Flea Markets

New York's world famous **Annex Antiques Fair and Flea Market** is a year round event with over 600 dealers. The section at 6th Avenue between 26th and 27th Street is open Saturdays and Sundays. The section between 24th and 25th Streets, also at 6th Avenue, is open Sundays only. Parent-teacher associations (PTAs) and churches may sponsor annual flea markets on their grounds as fund-raising events, selling donated items for bargain prices. See local bulletin boards.

Thrift Shops

Most neighborhoods have their local thrift shops. Such stores are run by churches, hospitals or charities receiving gifts to be sold to the public. These shops offer a variety of goods, including clothing, books, and furniture. Book hunters in particular may be thrilled with what they find. One example is the **Housing Works Thrift Shops** (at 143 West 17th Street and 202 East 77th Street), whose proceeds go to serve homeless people with HIV. One neighborhood with a heavy concentration of quality thrift shops is the Upper East Side between 80th and 86th Streets along Second and Third Avenues. The chain of **Salvation Army** stores represents another alternative. Aside from books, I haven't had much luck there.

Specialty Neighborhoods

Atlantic Avenue, between Nevins and Bond Streets in Brooklyn is known for its sturdy and functional furniture. Lower First

Avenue near Second Street in Manhattan is the appliance neighborhood. Household linens and fabrics coalesce on the Lower East Side on Grand Street between Forsyth and Allen. Canal Street between West Broadway and Broadway is an outdoor collage of hardware odds and ends, and the shopper has a quick escape from the Canal Street grunge to SoHo a block away. Kitchenware and lamps may be scavenged on the Bowery, in stores between West Houston and Broome.

Yard Sales

Yard sales are more likely to be found in the outer parts of the boroughs and in the suburbs. Yard sales and their rummage-sale cousins are advertised in the classified section of most newspapers. The elite of the yards sales are called "estate sales" and "moving sales." Classified ads indicate the addresses and times for these sales. A car is indispensable for covering various sales within a specific area so that you don't make a long trip only to find that the one sale you've jotted down is a dud. Individual items may be listed in such ads with phone numbers, so that you may inquire in advance. The best strategy is to get there on or before opening time, to beat out rapacious used furniture storekeepers.

Warehouse Outlet Centers

Many New Yorkers swear by warehouse shopping in Secaucus and Flemington, New Jersey, but others find these discount districts a hassle. You'll need a car to get there and a map to navigate from one specialty outlet to another. Those with more patience than this writer can find some of the same designer clothing and houseware brands for a fraction of the price of the same items back in the city. The best strategy is to get a friend who has already been there to take you. Warehouse outlet centers represent an alternative to the ubiquitous big-box, windowless shopping malls that plague most suburbs.

119

Sample Sales

These unadvertised sales are a means for designers to unload lefto-ver merchandise (furniture, jewelry, and other odd items) at the end of a shopping season. Word of mouth is the best method for finding these elite sales, although the "sales and bargains" section of *New York*, the city's upscale magazine, is a good source. Those who wish to keep up with the Joneses consumeristically will love these quality sales.

Auctions

New York's most entertaining shopping experience is attending an auction at **Christie's** or **Sotheby's**. Both of these venerable companies publish schedules of their events. Be there for the sale of a multimillion-dollar Van Gogh or the unloading of the goodies from the estates of famous New York historical celebrities. (See Chapter 9, for this shopping experience deserves coverage under the rubric of entertainment.)

ELEVEN WAYS TO STRETCH YOUR INCOME WITHOUT DIMINISHING YOUR QUALITY OF LIFE

Wealth depends not on the amount of one's income but on how much comes in compared to how much goes out. This chapter concludes with eleven simple ways to improve the ratio between what comes in and what goes out, without sacrificing on aesthet-ics or comfort.

1. **Buy used furniture.** Old furniture has an unfair competitive advantage over new furniture. New furniture companies survive only because of a stigma among many people about purchasing used furniture. But George Washington's two-centuries-old desk is worth considerably more than any desk produced today. Older styles of furniture are more intricate, with sturdier wood, and they're sometimes more functional as

well. Hunting for old furniture at New York's flea markets, rummage sales, church sales, and from private parties (through classified ads) is fun. Like their counterparts in Paris, New Yorkers legally dump their old furniture on sidewalks on designated bulk collection days. Call the Sanitation Department for the bulk collection day in your neighborhood and become a scavenger. Settle only for a product whose quality is equal to or better than what you get retail.

2. **When considering life insurance, it is better to purchase straight term insurance rather than any type of "investment" the insurance brokers will try to sell you.** You'll get a greater yield investing your stake (the amount of your money the broker would have invested) in a mutual fund of your choice, since the insurance company would otherwise keep its slice of the profits from your investment. Why let an opportunistic insurance corporation disenfranchise you from your investment freedom, especially when you're living in the investment capital of the world?

3. **Shop at farmers' markets and supermarkets** (as opposed to convenience stores or corner groceries). Not only will you save money, but your food quality will improve. With some of what you've saved, splurge on the city's specialty fish shops, bakeries, or international food boutiques.

4. **Enjoy New York's superb parks, trails, and sports facilities to keep in shape.** The savings comes later with reduced doctor and health care bills. Even if you do not engage in a sport, doing errands on foot instead of taking the car (in other words, purposeful exercise) will be of help in keeping in shape. Much of New York City is ideal for walking. New York's street culture is lively, the antithesis of the street boredom that plagues more automobile-dependent cities and typical suburbs. (See *Healthy Pleasures* by doctors Robert Ornstein and David Sobel for more on purposeful exercise.)

Walking across the Washington Bridge, with New Jersey in the background

5. **Enjoy New York's wealth of free entertainment.** We're not talking about an out-of-tune hippy strumming a guitar for coins. Many of the same musicians and theater groups that cost big money in their usual settings come out to perform for free on numerous occasions, as exemplified by Shakespeare in the Park and the New York Philharmonic summer concerts. (See Chapter 9.)

6. **Find the bank with the least minimum balance requirement and don't let your account fall below the minimum.** New York's bank menu is extensive and competitive enough to make shopping around worth your while.

7. **Pay off credit card debts before the end of the payment period.** Don't get burned by the steep interest rates. Any other type of debt is better than a credit card debt, except one with a vintage, knee-breaking New York loan shark.

8. **When you have the urge to dine in elegance, try the *prix fixe* lunches or dinners typical of many of this city's upscale restaurants.** Or, for a funkier experience, use word-of-mouth leads to hunt down out-of-the-way, family-run restaurants with reasonable prices, where the cooking is surprisingly good and the atmosphere homey. (See Chapter 5.)

9. **Use a MetroCard for public transportation.** After all, a single 7-Day or 30-Day MetroCard allows you unlimited use of subways and buses during the respective time periods. No more waiting on ticket lines, either. (See Chapter 3.)

10. **Find housing in one of the boroughs instead of Manhattan, or share an apartment.** Either option can cut housing costs in half; the latter option is especially for singles who are insistent on living in Manhattan. (See Chapter 4.)

11. **Don't use a car.** If you hate traffic but enjoy trains and walking, your most significant savings will come with not owning a car (or rarely using the one you own). This is a taboo subject in most of the United States, but many New Yorkers can identify with the concept of existence-*sans*-car, since they enjoy a superb public transportation system, easily accessible shopping venues and restaurants, and a tradition of pedestrian friendliness. The cost of an occasional taxi, Amtrak ticket, or rent-a-car for a vacation cannot compare with the cost of owning and maintaining a car. Other countries encourage their citizens "to experience life without an automobile." France's Ministry of Environment sponsors an annual "car-less days" festival to teach people that they can live without cars. (See Chapter 3.)

A Budget with Some Style

None of these budget-stretching devices involves penny pinching, and all of them are intended to improve one's quality of life. The money saved is money earned and can be set aside for those rare luxuries that truly fit within one's philosophy of life. Thanks to its immigrant economies, alternative cultures, and superb public transportation system, New York is a fertile ground for economical but quality entertainment and living options.

Chapter Seven

A HANDLE ON THE BUREAUCRACY

Multiply line 3 by 92.35% (.9235) . . . If the amount on line 4 is $65,000 or less, multiply line 4 by 15.3% (.153). Enter the result here and on Form 1040, line 47.

—Instructions on one of the simpler
Internal Revenue Service tax forms

The most fastidious bureaucratic obstacle for foreigners is getting to the United States legally. From then on, New York's bureaucracy is easy to handle. If you are already from the United States, you'll appreciate how complex it was for so many New Yorkers of foreign heritage to make it here in the first place.

IMMIGRATION

Foreigners who've acquired the addictive New York dream—maybe Woody Allen's Upper East Side version or the seedier *Midnight Cowboy* image—first visit the nearest United States consulate in their country. There, they receive free bad news about the many bureaucratic hurdles they must confront to enter the United States either as a **non-immigrant** (B1 visa for business purposes, B2 visa for tourism, or various other sub-categories) or as an **immigrant** (either through citizen or resident family members, or as skilled or unskilled labor in short supply in the United States). Those entering as non-immigrant students will require one of several types of "I-20" forms issued by their prospective school, and similarly, exchange visitors will be issued a Form IAP66 by sponsoring organizations.

Documents

Non-immigrants must present a passport which will be valid at least six months beyond the period of intended stay, a recent photograph 1.5 inches square, and, most importantly, evidence substantiating the purpose of their trip and their intention to depart from the United States. At this writing, 26 countries are part of a visa waiver program, including the United Kingdom, Ireland, Australia, and Japan. Inquire at your local U.S. consulate if your country is still on this list or has been added to it.

Potential immigrants should present a valid passport from their country of origin, birth certificate, police certificate, the results of a medical examination by a doctor sanctioned by the U.S. consul in their country, and, most crucial, evidence that they will not become a public burden once in the United States.

These are the encyclopedic requirements whose specific details are available through a U.S. consulate. But other tips, sometimes spelled out, sometimes between the lines, and sometimes unstated, are vital for potential visitors or immigrants.

Tips

Knowledge of the realities of immigration law and procedure before completing an application can save you from great disappointments farther down the road.

1. **For foreigners who plan on becoming immigrants, the best strategy may *not* be to first arrive as a non-immigrant.** Most permanent residency statuses will require the non-immigrant to leave the United States for a minimum of two years before returning with a permanent status. An exchange student who falls in love with the country and wishes to remain will have to depart for two years before a reapplication for a new status can be accepted.

2. **In the process of issuing a non-immigrant visas, U.S. consuls are equivalent to judges in a courtroom and legally may make subjective determinations in favor of or against an applicant, even when all required documents are in order.** The applicant's physical appearance and demeanor are vital during a consular interview. A consul could conceivably view

127

an applicant's "rough" hands and conclude that the applicant intends to work illegally as a dishwasher or fruit picker; or, he could listen to the applicant's spicy street language and assume that the applicant does not really belong to a social class normally engaged in tourism.

3. **The fact that foreigners are finally issued a visa does not mean they will be accepted by immigration authorities at the port of entry.** Suggestions on physical appearance and demeanor for the consular interview should remain in force during the interview with the immigration authority at the port of entry, and copies of all documents that served to obtain the visa should be on hand. A letter from an employer stating the non-immigrant's salary and date of return to his/her job, and a return air ticket will help the process of getting through this last obstacle.

4. **In the realm of permanent immigration, the United States attempts to weed out those foreigners who will not be beneficial in one way or another to the country.** "Preferences" A through E are clearly defined, referring to specific family relationships between the applicant and members of the applicant's family who are citizens or residents in the United States. But preference F, the labor preference, is based on job skills and experience specifically needed in the United States. Preferences under F are the "brain drain" preferences; the United States actively welcomes people distinguished in the sciences (being an Einstein helps), arts, education, business, sports (especially if you can throw a fastball at 95 miles per hour), and, in particular, executives from multinational corporations. If you plan to do business in the United States and are a successful businessman in your home country, you will fit within this latter category. Even with such preference, the quota limits the number of yearly immigrants under this category to 40,000.

Other categories with a quota of 40,000 are designated for members of a desired profession with advanced degrees. On the other hand, the quota for unspecialized applicants is only 10,000.

5. **Don't give up if you do not apparently qualify.** Consular brochures outline a category called "Special Immigrants" and another called "Refugees". For example, if you are a known opponent against a declared enemy of the United States (such as Saddam Hussein), you have an excellent chance to be admitted as a refugee. But if you are a known opponent against a brutal dictator who happens to be in good standing with the United States, refugee status is unlikely to be granted to you — even if your life is in danger.

The Fine Print

In a pamphlet issued by the U.S. **Immigration and Naturalization Service (INS)** called "United States Immigration Laws," there is a list of "Problems" (pages 10–11) which could hinder your otherwise impeccable application documents for non-immigrant or immigrant status. Most of these 33 "problem" categories are obviously necessary. But a few are of dubious concoction. Number 4: "You are mentally ill or homosexual" suggests (not my idea!) that homosexuality is a mental illness. Number 11: "You are a polygamist" seems to hypocritically apply to immigrants only, while polygamy among certain fundamentalist sectors of the Mormon community is tolerated within the United States. Number 28: "You are or were a communist or anarchist" would seem to bar, for example, a distinguished member of the French Communist Party who is a member of congress, even though this personality is accepted within the world diplomatic community.

I have worked from time to time with immigration lawyers and have also helped foreigners to obtain non-immigrant visas to the United States by providing unpaid paralegal advice. From my experience, I can say that your chances of successfully landing in the port of New York are greatly enhanced if (1) you carefully read all pamphlets provided by your local U.S. consulate; and (2) you explore all creative combinations that would enhance your probabilities of success. These pamphlets are remarkably detailed, so every possible avenue is mapped out for you.

THE LAW ON YOUR SIDE: STAYING OUT OF TROUBLE

If you are not a law-abiding citizen, this section will be of no use to you. But if you do abide by the laws of your land, you'll wish to avoid certain pitfalls that can cause good people to get into bad trouble.

Private automobiles

Many of the easiest ways to get in trouble with the law originate with a private automobile. **Liability insurance** is not only required by law but, in this litigious society, becomes a must for one's tranquility. Should you get into an auto accident, God forbid, even if it were not your fault, you still may be sued. Lack of insurance may lead to an aura of irresponsibility hanging over a driver who becomes involved in an accident whose blame is not obvious.

New York's infamous **parking tickets** are another nuisance. It is especially easy to get one of these expensive envelopes by parking on the wrong side of the street on a day when street cleaning was slated for that side, a regulation called "alternate-side-of-the-street" parking. Whatever the cause of the parking ticket (the fine of which will be listed on the envelope), you should immediately mail your payment, before days pass and you forget your infraction. After a month, your fine will increase $10 per day, and the markup gets worse as time passes by. With but one ticket, you risk becoming a "scofflaw," which gives the city the right to tow your car away to a pound, where it will cost you a minimum of $150 to retrieve it. (Should you suspect that your car was towed away by the city, call 212-TOW-AWAY to find out whether it was indeed a city marshal or a car thief who made off with your cherished vehicle.)

You may discover that your car was legally towed away, and that you did indeed have a parking ticket, even though you never knew about it because a drunk had removed it from your windshield or the wind had blown it away. The best way to avoid this spiraling nightmare is to ALWAYS TRIPLE CHECK THAT YOU ARE PARKING IN A LEGAL ZONE.

Needless to say, private parking lots and structures are extremely expensive, especially in Manhattan. If you see Woody Allen driving in a film, it's always in the Catskill Mountains or on Long Island. In Manhattan, he takes a taxi. For the $400 per month it may cost a commuter for a monthly parking pass in Manhattan, he or she could have used the same money for a more expensive apartment in Manhattan itself, thereby foregoing the need to park in the first place. Whole books have been written on parking in Manhattan, evidence that it's no simple task. (Out of obligation, we New Yorkers are the best parallel parkers in the world, and can fit into a parking space only one centimeter longer than our vehicle.)

Pedestrians are less vulnerable to legal tribulations than drivers. In California, jaywalking tickets are regularly issued, but New York pedestrians know they "can cross the street leisurely when the WALK/DON'T WALK signs are flashing 'DON'T WALK,' and can scamper across when the signs bear a solid 'DON'T WALK,'" according to Richard Laermer. When I once moved to California, taking my New York City street-crossing habits with me, I soon received two jaywalking tickets for infractions that no New York policeman would have dared call me to task for.

On the other hand, in California I never had to worry about getting sued because someone slipped on the sidewalk in front of my house on the snow *I should have shoveled*. This is a litigious society, so if you call repairmen to your apartment, make sure there are no booby traps that can cause an injury resulting in a law suit.

Paying Taxes

Another way to get in trouble with the law is to not pay your taxes, or, if you've had taxes deducted from your paychecks, to not file a return. Depending on how many "deductions" you've declared on your original W2 tax form at your place of employment, you may be required to pay more taxes before the April 15 deadline or you may be entitled to a refund. Either way, filing a return is in your self-interest. For the self-employed, filing a return may allow enough tax deductions to considerably reduce required tax payments.

It has become popular of late to blame the IRS for just about everything. Whole militia groups would have their followers believe that the IRS is somehow responsible for all the perceived ills in the country. But the Internal Revenue Service and its New York State and City counterparts are made up mainly of dedicated bureaucrats. Their job is just to collect taxes. Should you conclude that the tax system is unjust, as many of us have concluded in very different ways, this is the fault of the U.S. Congress and not the IRS.

IF YOU BECOME A VICTIM

Have you been wronged by an individual or an institution? Then take advantage of your legal recourses. In **Small Claims Court**, you may sue for as much as $3,000. In these "people's courts," no lawyers are involved, and only the evidence you submit to the judge will determine the merit of your case.

Should the offense against you be worth more than this amount, you may wish to hire a personal injury lawyer, referred to snidely as an ambulance chaser. The bad part is that such lawyers will ask you to sign a contract allowing them to collect between 33 and 40 percent of the damages you win. The good part is that you pay them nothing unless you win your case. They risk burning up lots of unpaid legal hours by taking cases with little or no merit, so, should they decide to take your case, you know in advance that you've been screened and can be optimistic about the results. The only way you can go wrong is by not providing your lawyer with accurate information.

Depending on the severity of your case, it could take from months to years to resolve. Your attorney, who is best found through word of mouth, will first try to settle the case out of court. If the opposing side is willing to agree on a settlement, it is better to accept, provided that what you'd have expected to receive is not so much greater than what they've offered.

Litigiousness in the United States has been under heavy criticism for several decades. Without a doubt, there exists a flagrant excess of law suits. Corruption among lawyers, doctors, and auto-repair shops (which I've witnessed first hand), is endemic, resulting in inflated settlements. On the other hand, the system works, and even undocumented immigrants have recourse to defending their rights as human beings under this system. I have lived in countries where no legal recourse was available and have seen people crippled by barbarous medical care or abused by government agencies without legal remedy.

The most attention-getting litigation at the turn of the century involves claims of sexual harassment. Don't let your guard down as Clinton figuratively and literally did with Paula Jones and Monica Lewinsky. Behaving with common sense toward the opposite sex could save you from costly and embarrassing law suits.

These are a few of the scenarios in which normally law-abiding citizens can find themselves in need of legal support. Other more obvious criminal activities need no explanation for readers who know the difference between right and wrong.

Discrimination

Should you find yourself in a position to hire employees or rent out housing, be aware that New York City has one of the most comprehensive sets of laws prohibiting discrimination on the basis of race, national or ethnic origin, age, sex, and sexual orientation, and you should be sure to follow the letter of the law in interviewing and screening policies. The **New York City Commission on Human Rights** (tel: 212-360-7640) will guide you to the right agency for proper forms to be filed for employers or landlords, and will also provide guidance if you feel you are a victim of discrimination. If you cannot afford an attorney, consult with the **Legal Aid Foundation** for referral to attorneys who work pro bono or for reduced fees. The legal referral service of the **New York City Bar Association** (tel: 212-626-7373) may also be of help.

INSTALLING UTILITIES AND OTHER SIMPLE BUREAUCRATIC PROCEDURES

Most of the other bureaucratic procedures for settling in New York are amazingly simple and efficient. In comparison, I recall my comical nightmare when my wife and I moved into our new (ancient) apartment in Paris. The day we moved in, the electric company was slated to connect its lines to our apartment. Coincidentally, within hours before the simple switch-flip was to take place, a wildcat strike broke out, involving only those electricians who set up new connections, and only in our neighborhood. We were the only ones moving into the neighborhood that day, so I asked the strikers whether their work stoppage was personally aimed at us.

"Don't take it personally," said one of the strikers with a smile. "This strike concerns our abusive administrator."

We thus lived for our first two weeks in Paris without electricity, and survived with the help of many neighbors. This will not happen to you in New York.

Power

In New York you'll wait no longer than one business day before your electric and gas service is installed, and you can trigger the operation over the phone, with no deposit required. **Consolidated Edison**, or Con Ed as we refer to it, can be reached by phone at 212-338-3100 (Manhattan), and, using the 718 area code for the other boroughs: 830-7400 (Queens); 802-6000 (Brooklyn); 409-7100 (the Bronx); and 390-6400 (Staten Island). For suburbs, see your community Yellow Pages.

Phone

For phone installation (if you don't already have one), purchase a telephone at any phone store. An example is **The Fone Booth** at 839 Third Avenue in Manhattan. (Renting from **AT&T** is expensive for long-term users). Then call either **NYNEX/Bell Atlantic** (tel: 212-890-1550) or **MCI** (tel: 888-624-5622) to compare rates and order the most convenient service. Once you've decided between the two, your company of choice will ask you a few questions to determine if they'll require a deposit.

As a consumer, you should be aware of the hidden costs of extra services like call waiting, call forwarding, voice dialing, calling cards with surcharges, and other gimmicks. When confronted with these choices, ask yourself if they are pure gimmicks, or if your lifestyle truly requires such extras. For example, if you often receive international calls, call waiting will require your friend abroad to needlessly pay for a call should you already be on the line with someone else of importance. Nor do you want to be put into a position in which you're obligated to say, "Well, could we talk about this multimillion dollar business deal later? I've got my veterinarian on the other line." An old-fashioned busy signal allows the caller to try again until the line is free.

You will next be asked to choose a **long-distance service provider**, deciding between AT&T, Sprint, and MCI. You may wish to make this decision ahead of time. All three providers have toll-free numbers. Compare their rates and services and make an educated choice. The same can be done with Internet providers.

Once you've made your decisions, your phone service will be connected within 24 hours, provided your house or apartment already has a phone jack (a 99 percent probability). This procedure has been slightly more complicated than that of electric and gas service installation only because you've had to shop around for the best rates and services. But everything has been done by phone, with no need to travel to an office and wait in line.

Driver's License

For your driver's license, if you have an out-of-state license in effect for at least six months, you stand a good chance to have both written and road tests waived. But you will have to visit your nearest **Department of Motor Vehicles (DMV)** office and take a simple eye exam, unless you can provide a report from an optometrist's exam taken within the past six months.

If your driver's license is from another country, or if you have specific questions, call 212-645-5550 for up-to-date requirements. Certain DMV offices have shorter lines than others. Find out by word of mouth. Whichever office you choose, it's always better to be there early in the morning for the shortest waits. Many DMV offices present the unusual and fascinating imagery of New Yorkers of all social classes being obligated to rub elbows.

Vehicle Registration

To register a vehicle, the process is more elaborate, requiring: completed registration/title application, proof of ownership, proof of insurance in your name, proof of inspection, sales tax clearance, proof of your name and date of birth, a bill of sale, and an odometer disclosure statement if your vehicle was purchased from a dealer.

This list is long, but it is comprised of simple requirements, and the process is as comfortable or more so than it would be in most other countries.

Library Card

To obtain a free library card—New York's most valuable document—just stroll to the nearest branch of the superb **New York Public Library** with any proof of address (utilities bill, letter written to you, etc.). You'll have your card in a matter of minutes. At that time, ask for a Telephone Reference Service phone number. Most reference librarians will go out of their way to guide you to the information you need, especially when you call or visit them in non-prime-time hours. Theorists who argue that government is less efficient than private industry will have a tough time explaining how government-run libraries in New York and much of the United States can be so remarkably efficient.

Trash

For trash pick-up in your neighborhood, phone the **New York City Department of Sanitation** (tel: 212-219-8090), and ask for recycling facilities and regulations applicable to your neighborhood. Simple regulations must be followed or you may be fined. Rinsed aluminum cans, and plastic and glass bottles are left in blue containers provided by the Sanitation Department, and newspapers and magazines are to be tied in stacks. Few people appreciate New York's superb trash collection system until there's a sanitation workers' strike and the garbage piles up.

Social Security

Non-citizens applying for the all-important **social security card**, which has gradually evolved into an ID card, should call toll-free at 800-772-1213 or visit the nearest social security office for information. Without a social security card, you cannot be

137

employed or file taxes. Non-citizens will need a birth certificate and/or passport, and the famous "green card" (alien residency card), which is really blue. Those here on a student visa can present their visa in lieu of the green card. A receptionist at the social security office will complete your application and you'll receive your card within a few weeks. Most social security tax payments go towards retirement benefits, which are outlined in free brochures from your nearest social security office. As with public libraries, social security is an efficient government-run system that has easily withstood the attacks of knee-jerk privatizers.

The Art of Waiting

These are the most important bureaucratic procedures for new-comers in New York. Someone wrote that "maintenance" in one form or another takes up 80 percent of our lives. The trick is to convert maintenance tasks into enjoyable activities. When waiting in offices, bring a good book or puzzle to solve, or talk to the people around you. Or use the waiting time to take a few deep breaths and reflect on the good things in your life, like being in New York City and dealing with one of the most fluid and least threatening bureaucracies in the world.

Chapter Eight

MAKING A LIVING

From Irish policemen to Korean grocers to Jewish jewelers on 47th Street, immigrants have followed their cousins and countrymen into ready-made professions—forging ethnic toeholds that have become part of the New York landscape.

—Thomas Goetz,
"Why New York Taco Stands Are Chinese"
from *The New York Times Magazine*

New York lures more newcomers than any other city in the United States, so it is to be expected that unemployment levels in New York tend to be higher than the rest of the nation. In 1997, New York's unemployment rate was 8.8 percent; by the end of 1998, it had dropped to about 7.5 percent. Meanwhile, the rest of the nation's unemployment rate was hovering at around 5 percent.

Europeans accustomed to higher unemployment rates of 12 percent (France) or 20 percent (Spain) will not be alarmed by the New York statistics. However, the unemployed masses in New York receive fewer social benefits and shorter terms for unemployment insurance than their counterparts in France. Unemployed workers who have exhausted their benefits are not included in the statistics. Furthermore, many New Yorkers, especially those inclined towards the arts, are semi-employed and engaged in the daily hustle for survival.

In order to elude the stiff costs of employee benefits, especially health care, certain employers are choosing to use an alarmingly high proportion of part-time workers. For example, 60 percent of New York universities' teachers are "adjuncts" (part-timers), but adjuncts account for only 15 percent of the payroll. It's "like it or leave it" for adjunct professors, who constitute just one example of a class of New York professionals who could go elsewhere to less-glamorous places and find full-time employment much more easily.

So if you've chosen to live in New York, you have also accepted the fact that it is apparently more difficult to make a living in this exciting city than it would be in a place like Houston, Texas or Omaha, Nebraska. But making a living is not only a question of finding income. It depends upon how much comes in compared to how much goes out. In sprawling Houston, for example, it is obligatory to own a car (or two, or three, depending on the number of family members). That means monthly payments for insurance, and for the auto itself, and a continuous stream of other expenses, including maintenance, parking, and tolls.

With New York's superb public transportation system, and with all-inclusive, mixed-zoned neighborhoods with all of one's needs within walking distance, one could conceivably live without a car altogether, and many New Yorkers have chosen this alternative. An automobile accounts for as much as a fourth of one's living expenses. So IF all other variables were equal, one who makes $60,000 a year in Houston, could maintain the same quality of life in New York on $45,000, and still rent a car for a two-week vacation to the Adirondack Mountains or Quebec.

Of course, all other variables are not equal. However, the point is that there are a number of ways to live well in New York on less income, depending upon one's choice of lifestyle.

Now that it's established that making a living is not simply the amount of one's salary or royalties, we can explore the various ways to bring in an income.

Essentially, there are three primary ways that New Yorkers make a living. The first and most obvious method is to get a job. Getting a job is not easy, but this chapter will offer a few helpful hints. The second obvious way to make a living is to start a business, and this chapter will provide you with the basics on how to plant and grow a business. Even immigrants from less affluent or impoverished countries find ideal niches in the business scene. Finally, there is a third (and less tangible) method for making a living, embraced by a large percentage of New Yorkers who have chosen to forge an artistic or anarchistic life by weaving a patchwork of income-generating freelance activities. Let's explore all three categories.

GET A JOB

To investigate which professions or skills are most in demand in New York I surveyed each and every specialty employment agency. My assumption was that if there were competition between three or more agencies *within the same job specialty*, such specialty jobs would enjoy a greater availability. Naturally, this methodology is not totally scientific. There could be one giant agency that monopolizes a certain profession. Nevertheless, the fact that various agencies compete for clients with the same skills suggests that the jobs these agencies specialize in may be more

141

available. A New York employment agency is not going to specialize in mountain-climbing guides, blackjack dealers, or automobile assembly line positions.

The result of this research is an alphabetical list of salaried jobs and professions which seem to be more in demand: administrative assistants, chauffeurs, chefs, child care workers, computer graphics artists, computer systems analysts, computer support technicians, data processors, domestic helpers, sales agents, and various technical personnel (temporary or permanent). Understand that this is a panorama of salaried employment. Interior decorators or financial consultants are not on this list because they would work from their own business or on a freelance basis.

Notice that absent from the above list is employment in a traditional New York mainstay: the apparel and textile industry. This livelihood has been hurt badly by advances in labor-saving technology and an increase in the exportation of production jobs overseas, where factory labor is cheaper.

On the other hand, publishing, another of New York's major employment sector, is on the rise. Book and magazine sales are soaring. But digital technologies make this a changing industry, and the market, too, has changed. Publishers of more elite products such as serious fiction or social analysis, are hurting. The quest for the best bottom line caused HarperCollins to discontinue Basic Books, its most thought-provoking subsidiary.

With the fame of Wall Street, you'd guess that financial services would be a major employment sector, and you'd be correct. However, this sector is extremely volatile, virtually handcuffed to the performance of the stock market. Every time the market turns downward, brokerage firms unload employees. A successful bond salesman, for example, can earn $700,000 a year, if he's willing to accept the drudgery. Brokers in more exciting realms of finance may love their job, which helps alleviate the obligatory overtime.

142

I've spoken to the spouses of "driven" brokers, and they fear for the health and well-being of their overworked husbands or wives.

"My husband takes his work with him on vacation and loses lots of sleep on cross-country trips for short meetings," one woman said. "I'd love to have more leisure time with him, but he's long ago forgotten how to slow down the pace of his life, and what can I do? He loves his job the way other people are addicted to a drug."

To finance, publishing, and apparel, we add one final sector of the economy that is most typically dominated by New York: tourism. The rise of both the stock market and tourism at the turn of the century at least partially explains the drop in New York's unemployment rate and a collateral drop in crime. But with the 1997 economic crash in Asia, a major source of New York tourism was temporarily crippled. Jobs in the tourism area are

Lower Manhattan — New York's center of jobs in the stock market, international banking, and municipal government, as viewed from the Staten Island Ferry

143

subject to fluctuations depending on the economies in tourism's largest markets. A downturn in any of the world's major economies could trigger the onset of troubled times for a number of travel-related industries in New York, such as restaurants, hotels, and tour agencies.

The best strategy for making a living in New York is to have a job waiting for you. Two valuable job-hunting resources may lead to the job you're looking for. The first is an Internet enterprise called **Jobs in the City** (website at *http://www.jobsinthecity.com*), which will cost some money but will save loads of time. This outfit posts your resume on an on-line database, a hit-and-miss strategy. A second option is *The Metropolitan New York Job Bank: The Job Hunter's Guide to Metro New York* (published by Adams Media Corporation), an annually updated guide with nearly 8,000 employer profiles, over 300 industry associations, nearly a hundred on-line career services, and 690 employment services.

A number of employed New York professionals told this writer that they got their New York job through the company or organization they worked for in their previous city or country of residence. These were the fortunate ones. The reverse process, getting sent *from* New York to your company's subsidiary in Kansas or Saudi Arabia, is a more likely prospect.

Ethnic Niches

Members of a lucky ethnic group can depart for New York with a ready-made job network awaiting them. A domestic nursing shortage in the late 1980s caused Manhattan hospitals to sponsor Filipino nurses, who were offered special H1-A work visas. Today, 10 percent of the city's nurses are from the Philippines, and 72 percent of female Filipino immigrants have been trained as nurses.

Whole volumes of jokes can be compiled about cab drivers who don't understand English and drive their passengers to Norwood instead of Northwood. New Yorkers will often gripe and groan that they can't find a cabbie who speaks English. But learning "New Yawk" English is no simple task, and you won't find unemployed New Yorkers lining up to apply for cab-driving jobs. They're not willing to face the stress and danger of being a cabby. Result: an implausible ethnic network has developed which brings together hometown rivals from their native lands — Muslims from Pakistan and Bangladesh in cahoots with Hindus from India. Technically, though, many of these cabbies are not employees, since they rent their cabs.

Similarly, Muslims and Christians from the former Yugoslavia, rivals in their own land, share the employment scenario of hotel housekeeping. Back in their homeland, the trend is nationalistic and monocultural, but the crosscultural background of these immigrant workers, who often know two or three languages, serves them well in the hotel trade. Before hypernationalist fringe leaders created separatist movements and Germany precipitately recognized Bosnia's independence, Yugoslavs from different ethnic backgrounds intermarried and were getting along fabulously. Today, the former Yugoslavia's ethnic conflicts could be settled by New York's brigade of hotel housekeepers.

Most of these housekeepers are women. With the city's stringent anti-discrimination laws, women should have earned the equal opportunity they deserve. The famous "glass ceiling" has risen to the top floor in industries such as publishing, where Jane Friedman, for example, took over the reins at the prestigious publishing house, HarperCollins. But subtle discrimination against women within some professions still exists. Women in search of employment will find a wealth of information at the **Women's Center**, located at 45 John Street, Room 605, New York, NY 10038 (tel: 212-964-8934).

Be aware that ethnic and gender-based income niches are not confined to salaried employment.

BUILD A BUSINESS

You don't have to belong to an exotic immigrant group to start a small business in New York, and in later pages, we shall see how a wide array of sources for financial, human resources, export assistance, subsidies, and valuable information is readily available to every New York resident who wishes to take the precarious leap into the business world.

But hidden within the official layers of business help are underground ethnic assistance networks. Some New Yorkers who fail to grasp the economics of small business become resentful of ethnic control of certain niches. But in reality, these ethnic groups often save certain American and New York traditions from demise. When the traditional diner business became unfeasible for New Yorkers with more ambitious business goals in mind, Greeks stepped in to save an American tradition. (Such ethnic business niches in New York should not encourage false stereotypes. Back in Greece, not many Greeks own diners. And don't expect the random Filipino in Manila to provide emergency nursing help.)

Besides, New York's ethnic niches often have little to do with cultural origins. What could be more traditional to New York than the hand-rolled bagel? But if we made the logical assumption that Jews would be the bagel bakers, we'd be dead wrong. Today, Thai immigrants are saving this New York tradition. They got their start in the 1980s when employed by bagel-chain stores. Now they've opened their own stores.

Mexican tacos do not have the heritage of Jewish bagels in New York. Given the recent influx of Mexican immigrants to New York, however, you'd assume that these Mexicans would open their taco stands. But in the early nineties, Fresco Tortilla was opened by a Chinese immigrant. The word spread in the Chinese community, and today, a New York taco stand is likely to be owned by a Chinese businessman.

My favorite small business in New York is the discount long-distance phone calling office. It costs between $10,000 and $20,000 to open one of these businesses, which offer discount phone rates, especially to Latin America. Most of the folks who run these businesses are from Santo Domingo, but long ago they've extended beyond the Dominican neighborhoods of Washington Heights and the Lower East Side.

With the mythology of gas-station hold-ups, and the decreasing profitability of the service station, many New York natives fled the business. Stepping in to help fuel-hungry New Yorkers were Sikh immigrants. Once you've had to fill up your tank a few times, you begin to suspect that the Punjab region of India, where these folks come from, must be overrun by gas stations . . . and that with all the nurses, the Philippines must have a great health care system . . . and that all Senegalese people know the exact time of day because they all seem to sell watches.

You don't have to belong to one of these specialty ethnic groups to have an excellent chance to start a business in New York and make it grow. Compared to other countries, and many other U.S. cities, the basic procedures for opening a business in New York have the bare minimum of bureaucratic nuisance. Let's go through a step-by-step procedure before elaborating on the many sources of business assistance.

Registering a Business

Corporations or limited partnerships register with the **New York State Department of State, Division of Corporations**, found at 162 Washington Avenue, Albany, New York. Call 518-473-2492 and they'll send you all pertinent information.

Partnerships and sole proprietorships—if doing business under a name other than their own (or "doing business as," a.k.a. D.B.A.)—must register with the **County Clerk's Office** in whichever borough of New York you plan to locate. But if you choose

147

to do business under your own name, you need not file with the County Clerk.

Only sole proprietorships with no employees are exempt from obtaining a **Federal Employee Identification Number (EIN)**, available through the U.S. Internal Revenue Service. Call their toll-free number, 800-829-3673, and they'll send you the forms and guide you through your application.

If you plan to run a sole proprietorship with no employees, thus far you've had not a single form to file. The only step for you and the final step for the other types of businesses is to obtain a **Sales Tax Number** by filing form DTF-17, which will result in your receiving a Certificate of Authority with your sales tax number printed on it, to be posted in your place of business. Call toll free at 800-225-5829 for the forms.

City Licenses

Visit or call the **Citywide Licensing Center** at 42 Broadway, 5th floor, in Manhattan (tel: 212-487-4444) to obtain a city license. When applying for this license, ask which State License, if any, you'll be required to obtain. General business activity also calls for a **Department of Consumer Affairs License**, but if you plan to be in a food-related business, you'll need a **Department of Health License** instead.

Financial Services and Business Assistance

There are too many business-help agencies and organizations to list here, so we'll describe just a few of the more strategic ones. For a comprehensive directory, check the city web site (*http://www/ci.nyc.ny.us/html/business/html/assist.html*). A sample of the incredible stories behind these agencies will better illustrate the abundance and depth of business help in New York.

The city's third oldest building, at 247 Water Street in Lower Manhattan, had become a boarded-up fire trap, scarring the block. Repeated attempts to salvage the historic four-story brick building had failed. Only St. Paul's Chapel on lower Broadway and the Morris-Jumel Mansion in upper Manhattan were older than this deteriorated heap of old bricks. The building's history was not at all glamorous; it had once been the scene of a tavern full of brawling customers who observed dog and rat fights for entertainment.

As a last resort for preserving the building, the Department of Housing Preservation and Development sold it for $1 to builder Frank J. Sciame, under the condition that he would completely rehabilitate the building. The builder put in $1.1 million to resuscitate the structure, within the strict historic guidelines of his preservationist benefactors. Other builders failed to jump at the opportunity since the result would be only four rental units.

If you'd like to live here now, near the Brooklyn Bridge, you'll probably pay at least $4,000 a month in rent. Meanwhile, Mr. Sciame gets a 14-year tax exemption.

About forty blocks north in midtown, things are happening on a grander scale. If you left the city a few years ago and came back to midtown Manhattan today, you'd hardly recognize it. And if you're a veteran of the area's seedier days and haven't yet returned, you won't believe me when I tell you there's now a Disney store in the neighborhood.

This is one of the city's designated **Business Improvement Districts (BIDs)**. The **Alliance for Downtown New York** (address: 120 Broadway, New York, NY 10271; tel: 212-732-2407), established in 1995, is attempting to transform this section into a 24-hour neighborhood—a safe community completely set for the 21st century. To do this, the Alliance is offering aggressive tax incentives to both landlords and tenants, drastically reduced utilities costs, and other goodies. The trade-off is that owners of this previously all-business district must convert a certain percentage of buildings or units into residential space. The

149

neighborhood's "Midnight Cowboy" days, with its XXX-rated establishments, itinerant missionaries, and the community of inveterate winos will be gone, to resuscitate in other neighborhoods like the district to the west of Penn Station. This is the famous 42nd Street, where, as kids, my friends and I would arrive from Queens via subway to experience the rough edges of life, which to us seemed much more interesting than our local shopping centers.

Giving business big incentives to clean up a district is probably a good idea, but not everyone likes what is happening around 42nd Street. One of the skeptics is Bill Talen, a guerrilla performing artist who had an anti-consumerism pulpit on Times Square. Now he makes incursions into the Disney store, shouting:

"Children, Mickey Mouse is the Anti-Christ."

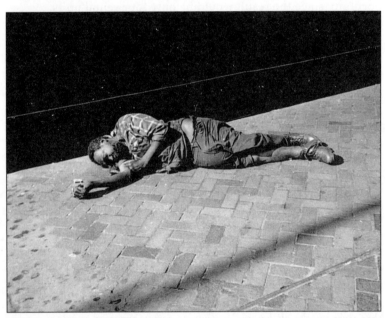

One of New York's unfortunate alcoholics who refuses to be relocated out of the gentrifying Times Square neighborhood.

This experienced actor developed his new persona to fight the "Disnification" of Manhattan, and has done a one-man show called "I Was a Tourist in the New Times Square," which re-enacted some of his in-store raids. He hopes that people will boot the corporate stores out of the neighborhood and "start conducting shady business in Times Square once again."

If the Times Square BID is the largest of its genre, then the Washington Heights BID may be the most creative. Aside from obtaining extra street cleaning, community promotions, and better access to government agencies, this BID "channels artistic energies to the benefit of the community." This Uptown BID has developed its own graphic arts department to help neighborhood merchants design catalogs or other forms of advertisement. Local artists are involved, and local printers get fed with paid projects in exchange for meaningful discounts.

The Washington Heights BID seems to have taken off thanks to the direction of George Sanchez, who coerces large entities in the community, such as banks, to buy from small, local businesses.

At this writing there are 37 existing BIDs—too many to list here, but if you're set to do business in any New York neighborhood, most small business owners will direct you to the nearest BID.

Beyond the neighborhood level are regional organizations helping people to grow their businesses. One such organization is the **Regional Alliance for Small Contractors** (tel: 212-435-6506; website at *http://www.regional-alliance.org*), a partnership of construction industries and government agencies which serves small minority- and women-owned businesses. Services include training, consulting, access to financing, and the matching up of small contractors with large companies.

One such small Queens contractor was Ms. Mamie Lum, whose BNG Construction Company (she is a co-owner) has gone from $1,000 gigs to some as large as $500,000, with the Regional

Alliance for Small Contractors playing an important role in Ms. Lum's sudden quantum breakthrough.

A similar service, called **Service Corps for Retired Executives (SCORE)**, provides free counseling on a walk-in basis at various locations. Call 212-264-4507. SCORE serves people who wish to start a business or those whose businesses are experiencing difficulties. I wondered how such a service could be provided for free. I found a SCORE volunteer, who explained that after having retired, he missed the business world, and felt rejuvenated with the volunteer work.

There are at least 30 different sources of advice and education for the small entrepreneur in the New York Metropolitan Area. But advice and education won't be enough without financing. Small entrepreneurs will find at least eighteen organizations that supply financing or at least lead you to the money.

The catch-22 in financing is that many non-traditional sources of money will want to see at least a year of a functioning business. "But how can my business function without a loan in the first place, and if my business is already functioning, the small loan you're offering is no longer what I need."

But it seems fair enough for financial boosters like **ACCION New York** (tel: 718-599-5170; website at *http://www.accion.org*) to require a year of business operation. Initial loans are from $500 to $1,500, made out to individuals or solidarity groups consisting of three to five entrepreneurs who guarantee each other. These loans go out to people who have been unable to obtain a loan from a bank or who have no prior credit history. Once the initial loans are repaid, entrepreneurs then qualify for larger loans of up to $25,000.

Current thinking among city administrators is that small business will do a better job than government in improving a neighborhood. With this in mind, the **Commercial Revitalization Program** (tel: 212-513-6436) can help you obtain a grant if your business will improve the neighborhood. This and other agencies may provide "matching grants," which simply means that they will match your investment. Many of these grants go to groups rather than individuals.

The best source for business people in search of financing is **New York's Financial Services and Business Assistance Website** (*http://www.ci.nyc.ny.us/html/business/html/assist.html*). If you prefer the feel of crisp paper, the best source of information for beginning and growing a small business in New York is the lively *Crain's New York Business*, a weekly sold at most newsstands with many of its issues dedicated to small business reports and guides for the beginner. Even those who do not plan to do business in New York will learn more about the city in *Crain's* than from the *Wall Street Journal*. The writing is sharp and entertaining.

GENERATE FREELANCE ACTIVITIES

Clearly, New York offers a favorable environment for starting a business, but the failure rate of small businesses still makes this a risky proposition. That's the negative reality. But with so many odd niches in this multicultural city, most good new ideas can find a new market.

Some folks are simply not interested in going into business. But neither do they want to be someone else's employee. These are people who wish to carve out a creative life, and perhaps are not as motivated to make lots of money, preferring instead to savor their daily existence by doing what they love. New York City can be both mean-spirited and compassionate to this type of individual, but clearly, the person who wishes to forge an artistic life will have a better probability of achieving his goals in a place like New York than in Springfield, Illinois or Dallas, Texas.

New York is the center of world finance, which can make the little guy feel even smaller, but it is also one of the world's capitals of the arts. This means there's a market for all kinds of unusual products and services. I once had a diminutive business selling Mexican bark paintings, along with a few watercolors of my own. I tried both Chicago and New York, and found it much easier to unload my merchandise in New York.

Had my escapade occurred a decade later, I could have been arrested. The city of New York has been attempting to regulate what it considers "an unwieldy proliferation of street artists" on a strip of sidewalk along Fifth Avenue owned by the City Department of Parks and Recreation. In September of 1998, the City decided to limit this activity, which took place in front of the Metropolitan Museum of Art. The order came down that there would only be 24 permits issued to street artists, at $25 per month.

The eclectic crew of Chinese portrait artists, Russian painters, Harlem photographers, and other niche artists got together to protest. About 50 painters, sculptors and printmakers protested in front of the Met, displaying unflattering effigies of Mayor Rudolph Giuliani. Four of them were arrested and handcuffed. Two were charged with disorderly conduct and the other two with inciting to riot. One of the artists, Sergei Rounovski, was hauled away with his baby daughter strapped to his back. The day the new rules took effect, artists selling without permits were issued tickets with fines of as much as $1,000.

Most independent practitioners do not face such difficulties in New York. For example John Laidman, a former sculptor, is now a metal fabricator who welds metal railings for stairs and balconies. Working as an independent contractor, he made about $35,000 in 1998. This was not enough to cover any health insurance, but by riding a bike instead of using an automobile, he lives as well as he chooses. The key word is "choose," for although Laidman makes $50 per hour, he chooses to work only one or two weeks per month, so his job won't cut into his playtime.

Laidman's profession is not so odd when compared to that of the "walker," a man—usually gay—who accompanies high-society women to cocktail parties and other events. Instead of a welding iron, the walker's tools are fancy cuff links and tie tacks. Essentially the walker spares the husband from social overload without being a sexual threat.

At the other end of the social ladder are French-speaking West Africans who sell designer watches on street corners from uptown to downtown Manhattan. It's a way of being independent, with low overhead and no fear of a layoff, and there's no language barrier in this gig.

Independence is the goal of many New Yorkers who do not fit within the business arena. Many of these creative souls are artists, attracted to New York's vibrant arts scene. The competition is fierce. Once upon a time you'd find these artists working as waitresses or bartenders. But the new trend is temporary labor.

"Temp" jobs allow artists to earn an income between exhibitions or stage roles. Some temp employment companies even specialize in artists. The average worker wants to be employed fulltime, but artists with the need for freedom prefer the temporary gig. Sometimes they work for a firm called Feather Dusters, doing cleaning. But some temp jobs are more closely related to the arts. **Professionals for NonProfits, Inc.** opened a division specializing in "art handlers" and, as of early 1999, has 115 parttime employees, all of them artists. They hang paintings, or organize museum exhibits or private collections.

Approximately 20 percent of the 1,500 temps sent out weekly by the TemPositions Group of Companies are in the arts, and they work at jobs such as speechwriters, computer workers, or receptionists. Many of the artists who do this temp work have been relatively successful within their art or craft, but need to supplement their income. There are no health benefits in these jobs, but nor is there any stigma about working for a only short period of time, and the jobs are readily available through these temp agencies.

One source of weird employment is found in the community throwaway newspapers. When I was beginning my career as a writer, I found a part-time handyman job in the home of a woman astrologist married to a wealthy plastic surgeon. It was a Zen experience painting her fence black and attempting to keep her black porcelain bathtub dustless. (Some of the cleaning was interesting, as I could caress her husband's glass sculptures.) The only dangerous moment: when I ran outside to separate the woman's dog from a lusty macho canine—since the potential mate was a Sagittarius, it was the wrong match-up for her Aries pet.

Today my New York work consists of freelance writing for magazine and book publishers, and a small tour enterprise. In the global economy, a freelancer is no longer tied down to a geographic location in order to earn a living. Readers who wish to live in New York and make their living on the independent track would do well to take some of their employment with them from other places.

New York's unemployment rate has been the highest of the 20 largest urban centers in the United States, and most of these other urban centers are creating new jobs faster than New York. But for the creative individual who prefers to freelance it, New York offers a wealth of quirky niches.

Should you prefer the less-wobbly path of stable employment, you may experience a degree of culture shock in typical New York employer-employee relations. Although all types of human differences exist within New York, supervisors tend to be forthcoming or blunt (depending on your culture of reference), as well as informal or lacking social graces. While some employers may seem rather tough, they're probably less likely to do you harm behind your back.

— Chapter Nine —

ENTERTAINMENT OVERKILL

In fifteen months, Disney will leave New York. I see a popular uprising. People will start ripping up the faux marble and start conducting shady business in Times Square again.

> —Bill Talen, a.k.a. Reverend Billy,
> from his one-man show
> "I Was a Tourist in the New Times Square"

What you won't see with us: the Statue of Liberty, the Empire State Building, Trump Tower, St. Patrick's Cathedral, or Cats. *Our feeling about those New York fixtures is this: get a map and see them yourselves in a day.*

> —Lee Habeeb, the "Real New York Tour" guide

157

New York City's entertainment scene is equivalent to a cluttered mansion containing thousands of consumer items, only 50 or 100 of which will ever be used by its residents. Shopaholics residing within the mansion have no time to use all the things they've bought. Yet outside the mansion are truckloads of other items begging to be purchased.

HONING YOUR APPROACH

Many newcomers fervently believe that they must conquer the city by partaking in as many possible forms of entertainment as possible. Such entertainment gluttony ultimate leads to a type of self-inflicted torture, the equivalent of force feeding.

The newcomer feels obligated to attend a **Broadway play**, for example, because it's the thing to do. Never mind that a recycled Broadway musical may not approach the quality or emotional impact of an off- or off-off-Broadway production that has less name recognition and presents a more authentic sector of the New York arts community . . . for a fraction of the ticket price. Such choices depend on personal taste. But many newcomers to the New York entertainment scene allow their personal taste to dissolve in the hype.

Taste rather than hype should also help in choosing of museums. The **Museum of Modern Art (MOMA)**, to cite one of my favorites, may not be as interesting for you, a medievalist, as the **Cloisters** in Fort Tryon Park, with its collection of medieval arts and architecture. If you had to choose between the two, would you choose the MOMA because you're supposed to see it, or would you opt for the Cloisters, which more approximates your personal persuasions?

In the realm of parks, few cities can compare with New York. **Central Park** is the "must," but even within Central Park, there are little known nooks and crannies that to insiders seem more appealing than the more highly-frequented quadrants of the park,

One of the many nooks and crannies of Central Park

(i.e., the ones you see in Woody Allen movies). Furthermore, who's to say that **Fort Tryon Park** on the Upper West Side (with a spectacular view of the Hudson River), or **Van Cortlandt Park** in the Bronx, or **Prospect Park** in Brooklyn might not offer you a superior alternative?

Music clubs present a similar dilemma, but multiply your potential choices by a few hundred, and consider all the unemployed New York musicians, some of whom are equally talented as those who have the top gigs. In the realm of jazz, as an example, the "must" club is the **Blue Note**, near Washington Square. But on any given night, the harmonies and rhythms at the **Audobon Bar and Grill** (Upper West Side) might be more appealing to your personal taste, or even of higher quality. A different choice would be the **C-Note**, billed as New York's best

159

sounding small room, on Avenue C in Alphabet City (Lower East Side), which charges zero cover but offers, on a given night, a more cutting-edge brand of jazz.

The sports sector of the entertainment industry presents an equally esoteric quandary. Is it worth sitting in the **Meadowlands** stadium on a cold late-Autumn Sunday if the **New York Giants** or **New York Jets** are facing an uncompetitive team, with the outcome likely to be decided by the end of the first quarter? This writer has seen all of New York's major pro teams (baseball, football, basketball, and hockey) play at one time of another, and can testify that the match-up between teams should be studied in advance in order to maximize the probability that you won't end up with a dull game. An early rout at one of these games would add insult to injury since you'll be contributing to the coffers of millionaire athletes who, for the most part, could care less that you're a fan.

There's no sport with greater sensorial impact (the crack of the bat, the color of the green field, the hum of the crowd) than baseball on a warm summer evening at **Yankee Stadium** or **Shea Stadium**. And the agility of **New York Knicks** at **Madison Square Garden** rivals the most graceful ballet. But if I had to choose the most guaranteed thrill in the most electric atmosphere for someone who has never attended any professional sports contest and may never again attend one, it would be a **New York Rangers** ice hockey game at Madison Square Garden. It's the fastest action in town and the crowd, of which you will be a part, represents one of the profound heartthrobs of the city.

Basketball connoisseurs interested in closer contact with athletes and the culture that surrounds them might derive a greater thrill from a watching a do-or-die **pick-up basketball** game in one of New York's cramped cement courts. These games are truly entertaining, and the unsalaried players take it just as seriously as their five-million-dollar counterparts.

Neighborhood basketball regulars draw a respectable crowd. It really doesn't get any more competitive than this.

This small sample of New York's entertainment possibilities is mentioned in the context of a discussion on the very difficult choices that must be made when confronting a bloated entertainment menu. The trick, if there is one, is to choose those few events or activities that offer the deepest and most fulfilling gratification over the many that offer passing moments of forgettable pleasure. The first step to accomplishing this goal is to forget about the hype, forget about trying to do and see everything, and concentrate on what you cherish.

Any week's entertainment menu would occupy this whole volume. The best strategy is to pick up a copy of *The Village Voice* or *The New York Press*, and study your alternatives.

161

FREE FRENZY

Despite its reputation for the most expensive array of entertainment options, New York is also the place with the most comprehensive and surprising menu of free events and activities in the world. Low-income New Yorkers may not get a fair shake when it comes to housing and food, but their consolation is state-of-the-art free entertainment. We're not talking about the Brighton Beach neighborhood band but the New York Philharmonic.

Some of the free events will be covered in the New York Calendar in the next chapter. An unabridged list is impossible, so we'll select a representative array from distinct areas of interest.

All of these places are listed in the basic phone directory, so only selected phone numbers deemed particularly strategic have been included here.

Arts

The city is brimming with artists, so expect to bump into a quirky array of galleries. A certain type of gallery sponsoring eclectic events as well as art exhibitions is labeled an "alternative space," the first of which, **White Columns** (tel: 212-924-4214) was opened in 1969 and stands at 154 Christopher Street in the Village. The **P.S. 1 Museum** (tel: 718-784-2084), at 22-25 Jackson Avenue in Long Island City Queens, is another of the original art alternatives. Nearby on Vernon Boulevard (eight blocks from the Broadway N-line el stop in Astoria) is the **Socrates Sculpture Park** (see Chapter 1). Other galleries include **Art in General**, found in a Tribeca warehouse and **Thread Waxing Space**, in a lower Broadway loft.

Beaches

This isn't Maui, but New York has its selection of funky beaches: **Brighton Beach** (a Russian immigrant enclave); **Coney Island Beach** (with its great amusement park and famous boardwalk); **Great Kills Park Beach** (a Staten Island nature retreat); **Jones**

162

Beach (on the south shore of Long Island); **Orchard Beach** (in Pelham Bay Park, in the Bronx); and **Rockaway Beach** (in Queens, with the most challenging surfing waves around).

Children

Beware! Throughout the United States, places advertised "for children" often trap gullible adults into unloading their hard-earned income for the privilege of waiting in long lines under the pounding sun for momentary pleasures with little (if any) long-lasting joy. But New York may be the most child-friendly place in the world. Give me a complete menu of children's activities from Orlando, Florida (theme park capital of the world), and I'll match it with an improved menu from New York — with the only difference being New York's lower price. (Do I sound like an obstinate New Yorker?)

I shall concede that Florida's beaches are more elegant than those of New York, but we have the **Coney Island** amusement park and boardwalk right on the beach. We've got the **Hayden Planetarium** and **major league baseball** (reasonable ticket prices), plus an astounding variety of green, forested parks. The **Alley Pond Experimental Center** in Douglaston, Queens, is the country in the middle of the city, with hiking trails, an aquarium, and recreational facilities. Around the medieval **Belvedere Castle** in Manhattan (near 79th Street) are nature, wildlife, and geology exhibits. The **Charles A. Dana Discovery Center** (at 36 West 110th Street) provides fishing rods and bait for fishing in the **Harlem Meer Lake**, and presents ecology exhibits and a Saturday performance festival during the summer.

New York has a number of children's museums, some free of charge and others with minimal admission fees. The list includes the **Brooklyn Children's Museum**, the **Children's Museum of the Arts** (at 72 Spring Street in Lower Manhattan), the **Children's Museum of Manhattan** (at 212 West 83rd Street),

163

the **Staten Island Children's Museum** (by Sung Harbor), and the **Sony Wonder Technological Lab** (at 550 Madison Avenue), all of which offer interactive and participatory activities.

Comedy

New York's greatest comedy events may be the arguments you hear in neighborhood parks and on street corners. But for more formal renditions of the art of comedy, several of the city's comedy clubs charge no cover, including **Luna Lounge** (in the Lower East Side), the **New York Comedy Club** (at East 24th Street) on Monday nights, and the improvisational **Solo Arts Club** in Chelsea.

Dance

Whether you do it or watch it, dance is an important part of the city's entertainment menu. Check out the **Young Dance Makers** (tel: 212-362-4740) for performances and audience participation workshops. Personally, I'd rather pay a cover charge and dance to a live band, but if getting on the floor and moving your hips is all that matters, a number of advertised boom-box discos charge only what you consume.

Museums

The **Whitney Museum of American Art** (at 945 Madison) offers free admission on Thursdays between 6:00 p.m. and 8:00 p.m. Other major museums have similar offers. In general, museums on the main tourist circuit recommend $8 "donations," but they do not expect a backpacker to pay the same as a stockbroker.

Just a few of the city's roster of quirky museums include: the **Ellis Island Immigration Museum** (access by ferry), the **Museum of American Financial History**, the **Lower East Side Tenement Museum**, the **Museum of African-American History and Art**, and **New York Unearthed** (great for children) which tells the story of archeological digs beneath the city.

Music

Mostly in the summer, but occasionally during other seasons, the **Bronx Symphony Orchestra**, the **Juilliard School of Music Orchestra**, the **Manhattan School of Music Orchestra**, and the **New York Philharmonic Orchestra** (Summer in the Parks) present free orchestral concerts. Jazz, salsa, reggae, folk, and rock music can be found at a number of bars, clubs, and cafes that charge no cover. At the Christopher Street subway stop, for example, one can choose between the **Groove** (rhythm and blues) and **Arthur's Tavern** (jazz). Music begins early at these places, and if you sit at a booth, you can even bring your non-drinking, underage minors to experience the type of music they're not exposed to amongst their peers. The **New School for Social Research (Jazz Division)**, presents concerts throughout the year, but especially during the winter holiday season. (For a calendar of events, call 212-229-5896, extension 305.)

With what you've saved with all this free music, you can afford to splurge at the Blue Note, which features some of the best jazz artists in the world. A Blue Note special is the Sunday Brunch and Matinee, which, for less than $20, gives you music, drink and brunch. Blue Note regulars include Grover Washington, Jr., Max Roach, Chick Corea, Nancy Wilson, and just about every other great you can imagine.

Theater

A good friend of this writer studied acting in New York. He would often work for free just to practice his craft, while earning his living outside his chosen profession. The quality of his acting was superb. With so much competition, many of the unknowns like my friend are just as professional and inspiring as the big names. Those actors and actresses who have been blessed with good professional fortune often remember the tough times and perform for free. At the **Free Theater Project**, 311 West 80th

Street, well-known actors perform in free monthly midday events. **Broadway on Broadway** (tel: 212-768-1560) is an annual free performance in September with acts and music from Broadway's current hits.

Be prepared to wait in a long line for the June performance of **Shakespeare in the Park**, at the Delacorte Theater, on the west side of Central Park at 81st Street. New York excels at creating alternatives to the alternative, and **Shakespeare in the Parking Lot**, at 85 Ludlow Street, is a less-traditional, but no less professional, rendering of Shakespearean classics.

A number of prestigious theater spots offer occasional free performances, including the **Gene Frankel Theater** (at 24 Bond Street), **St. Mark's-in-the-Bowery** (at 131 East 10th Street), **New Dramatists** (at 424 West 44th Street, for new and up-and-coming actors and playwrights), the **Ground Floor Theater Lab** (in Brooklyn, a place with a sense of humor), and **Theaterworks USA** (at Promenade Theater, on Broadway at 72nd Street; free summer performances with child-friendly settings).

This writer's strategy for catching plays is to not wait around for free performances. During any given week, just by consulting the *Voice* or *The New York Press* entertainment pages, you'll find an overwhelming menu of worthy off- and off-off-Broadway plays for a fraction of what it would cost you to see *Cats*. You'll have your choice of Beckett, Brecht, Chekhov, Havel, and other greats, or better yet, with synopses available, you can choose from among a wide array of contemporary dramatists who represent current waves in the New York drama scene. Overall, there are more than 100 alternative theater venues in New York, with a number of them charging less than $20 per ticket. If you look hard enough, you might catch a Havel play for $5 or a Beckett for $12.

THE ICONOCLAST'S ENTERTAINMENT GUIDE

The drama of New York is not confined to the four walls of a theater. Listed here are activities not usually considered "entertainment," but which can be fulfilling for those who in one way or another walk a different path.

Auction Houses

Try **Christie's** (tel: 212-546-1000) or **Sotheby's** (tel: 212-606-7000) for peeking in on New York's elite as they spring a few million for an impressionist painting or a piece of furniture from the George Washington era. But take care not to scratch your ear at the wrong time, or you may become the new owner of Mark McGwire's 66th home run ball, for a few million.

Cemetery Strolls

The French readily admit that their cemeteries are entertainment venues, especially the Pere-Lachaise Cemetery in Paris. With less fanfare, New York has equally seductive cemeteries, including **Brooklyn's Greenwood Cemetery** (with its trails, reliefs, and

167

period architecture) or **Woodlawn**, in the Bronx, where famous people like Duke Ellington rest among the landscaped hills.

In Search of Ethnic Culture . . .

Many of New York's more than 100 ethnic groups have their own cultural centers, with non-mainstream treasures, in the form of exhibits and performances. Within ethnic neighborhoods are local ma-and-pa stores with all kinds of odds and ends you'd never expect to see in the United States. My favorites are the *botánicas*, which are Caribbean religious stores that sell sculptures and carved wooden masks that would be the envy of ethnologists and art collectors. Don't miss the Haitian masks.

Screenings and Readings

If you're tired of the multiplex cinemas with the same car chase movies, try nontraditional film venues like cafés, bookstores, and libraries for avant-garde, foreign, and old U.S. classics. On Bleecker Street, one Internet café shows ongoing Chaplin films on a big screen. Try the **Donnell Library Center** (tel: 212-621-0618) for a schedule of movies. University student centers also post ads announcing free, on-campus film showings.

If you think literary events are for the stuck-up elite, try some bookstore readings by offbeat authors or better yet, a New York phenomenon: the poetry slam, a competitive literary event pioneered by the **Nuyorican Poets' Café** in Greenwich Village.

Inner and Outer Peace

The ultimate of alternative entertainment in this city of type-A personalities is to withdraw from it all and partake of type-B meditation at the **Himalayan Institute** (tel: 212-787-7552) or the **New York Shambhala Center for Tibetan Buddhism** (tel: 212-675-6544), both in eye of the south central Manhattan storm.

Should you prefer a less structured form of mediation, try New York's gardens. Among the many are the **Wave Hill Center for Environmental Studies** near 252nd Street (overlooking the Hudson River), the **High Rock Conservation Center** on Staten Island (that includes a garden for the blind), or **Fort Tryon Park**, Upper Manhattan, also overlooking the Hudson River.

The Ancient Art of Horse Racing

Once you're ready for the excitement again, partake of New York's race tracks. We've mentioned professional spectator sports, but horse racing is actually participatory. No, you don't ride the horses, but with the *Daily Racing Form*'s past performances, the analytical mind willing to put in some study can come out with a profit. By far the most aesthetic of New York's tracks is the stately **Belmont**, just across the border of Queens, in Elmont, Long Island (fall and late spring-early summer racing seasons). The Belmont's seasons alternate with those of the **Aqueduct** in Queens, which hosts races in winter and early spring. Both of these tracks feature thoroughbred racing and both dirt and grass tracks—as does the **Meadowlands**, just across the Hudson in New Jersey. North of the Bronx in Yonkers is New York's half-mile night harness racing track, **Yonkers Raceway**, although harness race betting is more predictable at the Meadowlands mile track (with fewer tight turns). A day or night at the track requires an investment in the form of admission, racing form, and program, so it is not recommended for those who plan to bet on their social security numbers or the colors of the jockey's silks. New York also has a number of **Off-Track Betting establishments (OTBs)**, not recommended because there's a 5 percent surcharge on the payoffs of winning wagers, and most OTBs are not comfortable venues. But they are still a fine place for stopping to observe New York's 300-year gambling heritage.

169

Sporting Spirits

Other participatory sports are considerably more strenuous physically than betting on horses. To handle the competition of **playground basketball or handball**, prior study of trash talking is recommended. **Cycling** is more serene, and New York's parks, bicycle lanes, and boardwalks are a cyclist's dream. Just about any pond will freeze over in the winter for **ice skating** (check posted signs for safety of the ice), but competitive skaters may prefer the hard-crunching **roller hockey**, which used to be banished to the streets but is now played under supervision in school playgrounds. **Baseball** is a New York tradition, but its easier counterpart, **softball**, is played co-ed, and you can even chug a beer during the game. **Stickball** is a street sport with the same rules as baseball or softball, except you need equipment for fishing out the "spaldeen" rubber balls from sewers. **Touch football** is a less-threatening form of tackle football and requires no protective equipment; but blocking in the lines can be ferocious. Hikers can go as far as they want by taking the **Long Path**, which begins by crossing the George Washington Bridge to the New Jersey side and then heads north through the Jersey's Palisades Park. Runners not up to the 26 miles of the **New York Marathon** will find many neighborhood 10K (10 kilometer) events to choose from — or you can simply run or jog in New York's numerous parks.

TOURS

The last thing you want is a fast-forward tour narrated by a chirping parrot. In general, the barrage of encyclopedic data from a tour is mainly forgotten within a day or two. But New York has various types of reality tours that involve the participant in the rhythms of city life or let you know the truth that's masked by the hype. (By the time you read these pages, New York's popular homeless tour guide, Timothy Levitch, will have probably graduated to other callings thanks to the film *The Cruise* made about his life.)

170

Discover Anthony Bowman

Virtually all foreign students registered at New York's universities will be affiliated with **Metro International** (tel: 212-431-1195), and therefore will be eligible to take the exciting walking tours of Metro's favorite guide, **Anthony Bowman**, a specialist in Black Manhattan. Bowman surprises his clients on the "Discover Harlem" bus-and-walking tour by proving, with a seeing-is-believing documentation, that Harlem is a "village of churches," with more than 400 churches in the neighborhood.

His "Discover Bronx" tour is no less dazzling, covering neighborhoods that encompass a wide variety of ethnic and national groups, including lunch in the Bronx's Arthur Street area, New York's most authentic Italian neighborhood.

Anthony Bowman takes foreign students on a tour of Harlem

New York's Reality Check

The "Real New York Tour," with guides **Lee Habeeb** and **Casey Magee**, covers the parts of New York "that most visitors never see, the part that New Yorkers use every day." Don't expect to see *Cats*, the Empire State Building, or the Statue of Liberty on this tour, nor the Museum of Natural History, which are "fine places, but you can find them on your own."

This is the anti-tour company. Habeeb and Magee take you to see artists at work, painters in their lofts, actors in rehearsal, even opera and ballet rehearsals at the **Metropolitan Opera** or the **Carnegie Hall Studios**. If the timing is right, you'll even see and hear rock bands close up, preparing for upcoming gigs, rather than watching them from a stadium seat where they're too far off to see with the naked eye. Write to Lee Habeeb at 14 Davies Street, Dupont, NJ 07628 for more information.

These iconoclast guides enjoy taking you to see New York's unusual workers in their daily setting, like fish mongers at the **Fulton Fish Market**, florists at the **Flower Mart**, or the whole-sale produce vendors at **Hunts Point**. Every social class is covered—the tour also makes its way to investment houses, the **Wall Street Trading Floor**, and the **Fashion District**.

Habeeb and Magee don't keep you walled up in Manhattan. "See the neighborhoods," they say. "See the boroughs." They'll take you, mostly by subway (since "that's how Real New Yorkers get around") to places like **Jimmy's Bronx Cafe**, **Sylvia's Kitchen** (a soul food haven in Harlem), a Russian dinner-and-dance club in Brighton Beach (Brooklyn), and a Greek restaurant in Astoria (Queens). At night you'll dance to live salsa and merengue bands, or if you prefer, visit a Baptist church in a mostly black section of Brooklyn and one of the many Orthodox Jewish communities in any of the boroughs.

"You've mentioned Jimmy's and Sylvia's. What other restaurants would you recommend?" I ask.

Lee calls **John's** and **Patsy's** the best pizzerias in New York. As for Jewish delis ("A community dining experience that is quintessential New York," he says), Lee recommends the **2nd Avenue Deli** or **Carnegie Deli**, the latter being a set in Woody Allen's *Broadway Danny Rose*. For steaks, he recommends **Peter Luger's** or **Spark's**. ("Forget Zagat's. We'll steer you right," he insists.)

Lee agrees with me on New York's professional sports teams (especially the Rangers) and beaches like **Coney Island**, but he

Don't expect to see the Empire State Building (left) or the St. Patrick's Cathedral (right) on the "Real New York Tour."

also recommends "**Chelsea Piers**. You can mountain climb, swim, play basketball, or golf there." Lee also agrees with me that "the best theater is often found off Broadway."

Like most New Yorkers, he has his favorite corners of Central Park. "It is safe, it is beautiful, and it must be used to be appreciated. Take a jog around the famous reservoir, the one Dustin Hoffman jogs around in *Marathon Man*. Catch some sun on Sheeps Meadow, or have a picnic at John and Yoko Ono's favorite spot-Strawberry Fields."

Lee's iconoclast stance is reaffirmed.

"We assume that you are all adults, and that, like most adults, you hate traditional tours, which is why we have no buses, no sweetheart deals with restaurants and theaters."

Real New Yorkers

Lee Habeeb and Casey Magee know New York and they know how to conduct a tour for people who hate tours. Both of them are denizens of New York's churches, ethnic enclaves, and after-hour bars.

Lee Habeeb practiced for his anti-tour enterprise by showing the town to friends. "Pretty soon, people we hardly knew were asking for a day or two at a time," he says. Lee's first contact with the city was as a basketball player. He competed successfully with New York players and then adopted the city as his own. He also spent years studying at Uta Hagen's prestigious acting school. His eclectic background includes work in the music industry and articles and columns on culture and politics for important magazines and newspapers. He studied law and economics at the University of Virginia Law School, which gave him contacts with some of New York's largest law firms and investment banking houses.

Casey Magee is a lifelong resident of Brooklyn. Her international traveling, mainly in South America and Europe, has helped her become a specialist on New York's ethnic neighborhoods. Having taught in inner city schools, she is in tune with the city's youth culture. As an extraordinary dancer, Casey can guide you to the best dance halls. She can also locate the best pastrami sandwich and the most intriguing wine list.

I first heard about Lee and Casey from a close friend who had taken their tour and had sworn by it. It seemed as if their affinity for "the real New York" was a perfect match for the objectives of this book.

The Real New York Tour helps confirm my belief, as a native New Yorker, that I'd be wasting pages by regurgitating information about my city's most obvious entertainment and visitors' attractions, which after all are ubiquitous features in every free tourist brochure. Definitely see the Empire State and Chrysler Buildings though. You'll have no trouble whatsoever finding them. Just look up.

THE OVERKILL CONTINUES . . .

Some activities and attractions not mentioned in this chapter belong to the special genre called annual events, which deserves its own chapter entirely, as New York City's entertainment gluttony continues on.

CHAPTER TEN

MENU OF SPECIAL EVENTS

New York's excitement resides in the daily and nightly rhythms of the city. One could live a fulfilling life without ever attending any of the city's annual festivals. Many New Yorkers have never been to the St. Patrick's Day Parade on March 17 nor rubbed elbows with the throngs at the New Year's Eve street celebration at Times Square.

But for every sensible logic there is an opposite sensible logic. A lover of festivals could spend a whole calendar year hopping from one annual celebration to another with few if any periods to take a break. And the good news is that most of these annual rituals are free of charge. In New York, one can live a full life without any of these festivals, fairs, and parades, or on the contrary, one can embark on a frenetic odyssey through a yearlong calendar of incomparable events. Children and adolescents will never be able to tell their parents they have nothing to do.

Strategically, festival lovers will be better off living within the five boroughs or just across the Hudson River in New Jersey. The nearer you are to Manhattan, the more accessible is the excitement. All events and festivals listed are free, unless otherwise indicated. And unless a different borough is noted, all events are in Manhattan. Check any local newspaper for specific dates, or you can call the **Parks and Recreation Department, Special Events** (tel: 212-360-8146) or the **New York Convention and Visitors Bureau** (tel: 212-397-8222).

JANUARY

Winter Festival, in Central Park, is a way to warm the heart and brighten the soul on cold, gloomy afternoons. **Chinese New Year** (at the end of January or beginning of February in Chinatown) is New York's only ethnic festival that dares to take the streets in the midst of winter.

FEBRUARY

Black History Month, an eclectic array of events throughout the city, rescues New York from its most dreary month. Meanwhile, the **Westminster Kennel Club Dog Show** (entrance fee required) is Madison Square Garden's alternative for those not so inclined to the action of basketball and hockey.

MARCH

New York begins to thaw out in March—not a month known for a great number of public events. But one event alone makes the month: the **St. Patrick's Day Parade**, making its way down Fifth Avenue (between 44th and 86th Streets) on March 17.

Although of less historical tradition, the **Greek Independence Day Parade**, which heads down Fifth Avenue (between 49th and 59th Streets) on March 25, commemorates an ethnic group that has done much to preserve many aspects of Americana that

177

were threatened with extinction, like the ma-and-pa coffee shop and diner.

Fauna and flora exhibitions during this month include the **International Cat Show** at Madison Square Garden (entrance fee required), the Horticultural Society's **New York Flower Show** at Pier 92, and to top it all off, **Earth Day** (in mid-March), with idealistic street celebrations throughout the city.

APRIL

With the onset of warm afternoons and the true beginning of spring, April's events are usually rooted in seasonal traditions, such as the **Easter Parade** on Fifth Avenue (between 44th to 59th Streets), the **Cherry Blossom Festival** at the Brooklyn Botanical Garden, and the **opening of the baseball season** (admission fee required). Yankees fans head to **Yankee Stadium** in the Bronx,

Waiting for autographs from their favorite baseball players, Yankee fans settle for the signature of popular sports broadcaster Russ Salzberg.

while Mets fans make **Shea Stadium** in Queens their second home. For baseball enthusiasts, April is always a time of great expectations, when the hopes for hometown teams are running high. Both the thawing spring weather and the uncertainty of the long season ahead make April one of the best times to see a ball game.

For a more mellow event, try the **Grammercy Park Flower Show** at Grammercy Park.

MAY

May is perhaps the month with the most eclectic array of festivals. If you attend the **Ninth Avenue International Food Festival**, between 37th and 57th Streets, bring enough money to try a variety of foods. Some advice: don't eat the first thing you see. First check out the outdoor menu in order to avoid becoming full before you discover the best dishes.

Other events in May present a generous slice of New York personality. The long list includes **Brooklyn Bridge Day**, during the second week of May; the **Martin Luther King, Jr. Day Parade**, on Fifth Avenue (between 44th and 86th Streets) on the third Sunday of May; the **You Gotta Have Park** celebration in various city parks (including, of course, Central Park); the **Washington Square Outdoor Art Exhibit** during the last week of May; and the **Bronx Week Parade** on East Tremont Street in late May (sometimes early June). And if the New York Knicks (basketball) or the Rangers (hockey) have made the play-offs of their respective leagues, then **Madison Square Garden** becomes a hot spot in the month of May.

JUNE

For travelers on a tight budget who have an affinity for elite culture, June is the month to see New York. The **Museum Mile Festival**, on Fifth Avenue (between 82nd to 105th Streets) in mid-June, is more than just a street festival—there's also free admis-

179

sion to the **Metropolitan Museum of Art**. During the same period, you can enjoy the **Metropolitan Opera Parks Concerts** in several parks around the city. If that's not enough, June kicks off the **Shakespeare in the Park** series at the Delacorte Theater in Central Park. The series lasts through August, but pick up tickets early (tel: 212-861-7277).

Central Park is also the location of a series of free concerts by the **New York Philharmonic Orchestra**. Like the Shakespeare in the Park series, tickets are on a first-come-first-serve basis, so call early (tel: 212-875-5709). The Philharmonic concerts are scheduled through August. Also beginning in June (and lasting through July) is the **JVC Jazz Festival**, which moves to various locations throughout the city.

For parade-watchers, June is a busy month highlighting some of New York's most traditional cultural sectors. Check out the **Salute to Israel Parade** on Fifth Avenue (between 52nd and 79th Streets) in the first week of June; the **Puerto Rican Day Parade**, on Fifth Avenue (between 44th and 86th Streets), also in the first week of June; the **Philippines Independence Day Parade**, on Madison Avenue (between 26th and 41st Streets) in mid-June (Filipinos share some history with Puerto Rico as both of these island cultures fell under U.S. control in the wake of the 1898 Spanish-American War); and the **Gay and Lesbian Pride Day Parade**, on Fifth Avenue (from 59th Street to Washington Square). The gay liberation movement began in Greenwich Village, so this last parade is of historical significance. Queens has its own version in Jackson Heights in the first week of June.

If patriotism is not your thing, but you like parades, then you can try the **Mermaid Parade**, on Coney Island in Brooklyn, or the **Coney Island Parade** at Steeplechase Park, also in Brooklyn.

June is also a month of street fairs. Among the best are the **Second Avenue Festival** (in the first week of June), and the **Feast of Saint Anthony of Padua** (also in the first week of June), on

Sullivan Street (south of Houston Street) in Greenwich Village. Children will especially enjoy **Kidsday**, a festival sponsored by the Brooklyn Historical Society and the Brooklyn Public Library.

JULY

A number of the June events continue on into July, August, and even September. As we continue to enjoy Shakespeare in the Park, the New York Philharmonic Park Concerts, and the JVC Jazz Festival, we can also hop around to various locations to watch street entertainers at the **Buskers Fare Festival**, sponsored by the **Lower Manhattan Cultural Council** (tel: 212-432-0900). Similarly, the ongoing **Washington Square Music Festival**, which begins in June, reaches its peak in July.

One festival that attempts to cover the whole spectrum of art genres is the **Celebrate Brooklyn Annual Festival**, which takes place in the Prospect Park Bandshell and includes music, dance, theater, and film. The events begin in June and extend through August.

Fireworks and street festivals are the staples of the United States' **Independence Day** on July 4. Two of New York's premier locations for Independence Day celebrations are the edge of the East River (where you can catch a good view of the **Macy's 4th of July Fireworks**) and the **Water Street July 4th Festival** (between State and Fulton Streets).

More music in July, free of charge: the **Summergarden free concerts**, the **Museum of Modern Art**, and the **MacIntosh Music Festival** throughout downtown.

Have you begun to feel guilty about experiencing all this culture and festivity without having to shell out a cent? Then it's time to dip into your savings and pay for the **Mostly Mozart Festival** at Lincoln Center. Too bad Mozart receives no royalties.

AUGUST

The cultural frenzy continues as many of the concert and drama series already mentioned spill over into August. The Indians and the Pakistanis may have their disagreements back in Asia, but here in New York City, they have back-to-back celebrations: the **Indian Day Parade** and the **Pakistan Independence Day Parade**, both on Madison Avenue, between 26th and 41st Streets.

Other ethnic-flavored festivities include the **Puerto Rican Day Parades** (in Bronx and Brooklyn) and **Harlem Week**, occurring in mid-August with ongoing music, dance, and art.

For a break from the "culture" scene, try catching a match or two at the **U.S. Open Tennis Tournament** (admission fee required) in Flushing, Queens. The last grand slam tournament of the professional tennis tour, the U.S. Open attracts the top players in the world—plus a number of famous New York celebrities who love to watch the game.

SEPTEMBER

Don't become festivaled out before September, New York's most bizarre month of events. For starters, the **baseball pennant races** are heating up, and if the Yankees and/or Mets are still alive for a potential spot in the end-of-season play-offs, suddenly the tension mounts. Unlike Shakespeare in the Park, whose dramas have predetermined endings, the drama of Major League Baseball "ain't over til it's over," as the former Yankee great, catcher Yogi Berra once said.

Although baseball is still the American pastime, the New York Menu never sticks to one dish, and September happens to dish up a smorgasbord of fascinating international festivals, including the **West Indian Carnival**, known for its spirited dancing and bizarre costumes; the **Feast of San Gennaro**, a ten-day fair on Mulberry Street (in Little Italy) that conjures up the Italian neighborhood of old; and the **One World Festival**, a shindig of mega-multicultural proportions held on East 35th Street (between First and Second Avenues) in the second week of September.

Like baseball, the New York parade season "ain't over till it's over." Major parades in the month of September include the **Von Steuben Day Parade**, a celebration of German culture that marches down Fifth Avenue, between 61st and 86th Streets; the **African American Day Parade**, proceeding along Adam Clayton Powell Boulevard, from 111th to 142nd Streets; the **Korean-American Parade**, which extends from 41st Street at Broadway to 23rd Street; and the cross-cultural **African American and Caribbean Parade**, syncopating through the Bronx on Tremont Avenue. The **Labor Day Parade** on Fifth Avenue (between 33rd to 72nd Streets) marks the end of summer vacation.

New York's street fairs continue with the **Third Avenue Street Festival**, between 68th and 96th Streets. For the Broadway-minded, **Broadway on Broadway** at Times Square has Broadway performers departing from their theaters to perform some of their favorite songs from Broadway musicals.

September is also ripe with celebrations of more niche subcultures, such as **Wigstock**, a Labor Day festival of drag queens. More sedate events include **New York is Book Country**, a book fair on Fifth Avenue, between 48th and 59th Streets; the **Harvest Fair** at the Brooklyn Botanic Garden; and the **Richmond County Fair**, a joyous Labor Day event on Staten Island.

Both the **Metropolitan Opera season** (at Lincoln Center) and the **pro football season** (at the Meadowlands, the home stadium of both the New York Jets or the New York Giants) kick off in September—book your tickets early.

OCTOBER

October marks the opening of the **ice skating season** at Rockefeller Center and in Central Park (with paid admission). With the weather changing from mellow to melancholy, a good parade can lift the spirits—and you have a bunch to choose from. Take your pick among the **Columbus Day Parade** (on Fifth Avenue, between 44th and 86th Streets), the **Hispanic Day Parade** (on Fifth Avenue, between 44th and 72nd Streets), the **Pulaski Day Parade** (on Fifth Avenue once again, between 26th and 52nd Streets), the **Italian-American Parade** (along 18th Avenue in Brooklyn), and the most bizarre of all these events, the **Halloween Parade** (on Sixth Avenue, between Union Square Park and Spring Street, in Greenwich Village).

October is also the month of one of the world's great participatory sports events, the **New York City Marathon**, usually held in the last week of October (sometimes at the beginning of November). Check out the view of thousands of runners from any park-overlook above the George Washington Bridge, or train for a year and enter the race by calling the **New York City Runners Club** (tel: 212-860-4455).

The autumn nip in the air invigorates the October street festival scene, which includes the **Columbus Avenue Festival**, the **Lexington Avenue Oktoberfest**, the **Columbus Day Fair**, the **Second Avenue Autumn Jubilee**, and the **Promenade Art Show** in Brooklyn Heights.

NOVEMBER

By now you won't ever again want to witness a parade. But two of New York's most traditional parades are held in the cool November weather: the **Veterans Day Parade** (on Fifth Avenue, between 24th and 39th Streets) and the **Macy's Thanksgiving Day Parade** (from 79th Street on the west side of Central Park all the way to 34th Street).

November marks the opening of the winter season of the **New York City Ballet** at Lincoln Center, plus another ballet season in Madison Square Garden: **professional basketball**. Catch the New York Knicks as they take a shot at the NBA (National

Basketball Association) title. Both ballet and basketball require advance ticket purchase.

DECEMBER

The great event of this month is the **New Year's Eve Celebration and Ball Drop in Times Square**, a sad time for those who do not wish to remember that time is passing by at a fast clip. By mid-December, it gets dark before 4:30 p.m., so lights act as a psychological substitute for the sun. Light-show events include: the **Christmas Tree-Lighting Ceremony** at Rockefeller Center, eight nights of the **Lighting of the Hanukkah Menorah** at the Grand Army Plaza in Brooklyn, and the **New Year's Eve Fireworks** in Central Park.

Lights can only offer psychological warmth, but the **Midnight Run** in Central Park will illustrate how the body, with the help of the mind, can overcome the cold. Or, head indoors and buy a ticket for the **New York Philharmonic's New Year's Eve Concert**, a stirring event.

THAT'S ALL?

In addition to the New York events just mentioned, every city and town in nearby New Jersey and the suburbs in Long Island, Westchester County, and Connecticut hosts its own local festivals. But the nearer you are to Manhattan, the more frequent and frenetic are the impressive annual events. With so much happening, it is no wonder that a hard core of inveterate New Yorkers, in their international setting, become so provincial and decide that "we've got everything so why go elsewhere?"

INTERACTIVE DIRECTORY

Many phone numbers and addresses are already included within the text. This directory will highlight a few of those most essential contacts for becoming a participant in New York life, and also add some new sources that did not fit neatly within the text but are of great strategic value for both short- and long-term visitors. Three-digit area codes presented in this directory and in the text should be preceded by the digit "1." When making a local call, the area code is omitted altogether. Manhattan's area code is 212. The other boroughs are all within the 718 area code. Directory information may be reached by dialing 411.

The universal toll-free **emergency number for police, fire, or health emergencies** is 911. The horror stories of 911 operators asking a victim for his life story while the knife-wielding burglar goes in for the kill are mainly fiction.

All phone or fax numbers and street or e-mail addresses were updated as near as possible to publication time of this book. The author cannot be responsible for subsequent changes in locations and contact numbers of any organizations or establishments listed here or within the text.

ALL-PURPOSE PHONE NUMBERS

- The **New York Convention and Visitors Bureau** is the strategic source of information or referrals: 212-397-8222.
- **Doctors on Call**: 212-737-2333 or 718-238-2100.
- **Legal Referral, New York Bar Association**: 212-626-7373.
- **Travelers Assistance**: 212-944-0013.
- For utilities problems, contact **Con Edison**: 212-683-0862 for electrical emergencies, and 212-683-8830 for gas emergencies.

BUSINESS

Doing business will automatically qualify you as a participant in the city's life and open doors to meeting New Yorkers.

- A list of all **City Programs of Financial Services and Business Assistance** can be accessed via Internet at:
  http://www.ci.nyc.ny.us/html/business/html/assist.html
- For the **City Business Assistance Program**, call: 212-618-8810.
- All pertinent **contacts for registering a business** are available via Internet at:
  http://www.ci.nyc.ny.us/html/business/html/reg-bld.html
  This site lists the phone numbers for registering various categories of businesses; it also indicates the necessary contacts for **Internal Revenue Service (IRS)** requirements and **Sales Tax Numbers**.
- Tip: Sole proprietors doing business under their own name are not required to file with a **County Clerk**, nor must they register with the State of New York.

187

- The weekly *Crain's New York Business*, available on newsstands, (website at *http://www.crainsnewyork.com*) is must reading for anyone interested in doing business in New York City.
- Immediate contact with **Chambers of Commerce** may guide business-oriented newcomers to the right source for their specific referrals. E-mail contacts include: *np@manhattancc.org* (Nancy Ploeger of the Manhattan Chamber of Commerce); *chamber@bronxmail.com* (the Bronx Chamber of Commerce); *info@sichamber.com* (the Staten Island Chamber of Commerce); *brooklynchamber@worldnet.att.net* (the Brooklyn Chamber of Commerce); and *queenschamber@worldnet.att.net* (the Queens Chamber of Commerce).

Business Licenses

City and/or state licenses will be necessary for most business operations.

- Check the New York City website for all pertinent **contact information on business licences**: *http://www.ci.nyc.ny.us/html/business/html/licenses.html* This website will also allow you to download *Licenses, Permits, Certificates & Applications — Where to Apply*, which is a chapter contained in the *Green Book . . . The Official Directory of the City of New York*. The *Green Book* is available at CITYBOOKS STORE, 1 Centre Street, Room 2223, New York, NY 10007 (tel: 212-669-8246/8247).
- For city licenses, write or visit the **Citywide Licensing Center** at 42 Broadway, 5th Floor, New York 10002, or you can call 212-487-4444.
- For a state license, fax a request for an application to the **New York State Department of State, Division of Corporations**, at 518-473-6648 (or call 212-417-5747) if you think that your business may be under the jurisdiction of other departments such as Agriculture, Liquor, etc.

CONTINUING EDUCATION

When you take a non-credit continuing education course, you are assured of belonging to a group of mature individuals who share a common interest. People take these courses for no other motive than personal commitment. Continuing education courses are natural scenarios for the development of lasting friendships and partnerships. Some of New York's continuing education settings are listed here. An asterisk indicates low-tuition schools with the greatest variety of offerings. Also included are a few interesting professional schools with more long-term programs. Important: another source of adult evening courses is the nearest community college; ask for their "continuing education" department.

- **Baruch School of Adult and Continuing Education**, 48 East 26th Street, New York, NY 10010 (tel: 212-802-2000).
- **Brooklyn Botanic Garden**, 1000 Washington Avenue, Brooklyn, NY 11225 (tel: 718-622-4433) for botany lovers.
- **Brooklyn Conservatory of Music**, 58 Seventh Avenue, Brooklyn, NY 11217 (tel: 718-622-3300).
- *****Borough of Manhattan Community College**, Office of Continuing Education, 199 Chambers Street, New York, NY 10007 (tel: 212-346-8000).
- *****Brooklyn YMCA**, 30 Third Avenue, Brooklyn, NY 11217 (tel: 718-875-1190).
- **Inwood Community Services**, 651 Academy Street, New York, NY 10034 (tel: 212-942-0043).
- **Juilliard School of Music**, Lincoln Center Plaza, New York, NY 10023 (tel: 212-799-5000).
- **New School of Social Research**, 66 West 12th Street, New York, NY 10011 (tel: 212-229-5600), a vanguard institution for understanding social realities.
- **Pratt Institute**, Continuing Education, 200 Willoughby Avenue, Brooklyn, NY 11205 (tel: 718-636-3453).

- *Stuyvesant Adult Center, 345 East 15th Street, New York, NY 10003 (tel: 212-254-2890), one of the most eclectic and inexpensive adult education centers.
- Third Street Music School Settlement, 235 East 11th Street, New York, NY 10003 (tel: 212-777-3240).

SPORTS

Participation in team sports creates a scenario for instant camaraderie. Choose your favorite sport and you'll soon become part of the scene.

- The three best information sources for all sports facilities are: The Department of Parks and Recreation (tel: 212-408-0209); the Chelsea Piers Sports and Entertainment Complex on the Hudson River at 23rd Street (tel: 212-336-6500); and the city's network of YMCAs, including McBurney YMCA (tel: 212-741-9210), which boasts a swimming pool, a full-sized basketball court, and an indoor jogging track, plus facilities for gymnastics, weight lifting, handball, volleyball, and fencing.
- Many fee-charging clubs, open to the public, sponsor organized sports. The Cosmopolitan Soccer League (tel: 201-861-6606) organizes outdoor amateur leagues, while Chelsea Piers (tel: 212-336-6500) sponsors indoor leagues.
- The New York Road Runners Club (tel: 212-860-4455) holds the unwieldy New York Marathon and more than 100 other less glamorous but more intimate races. Billiards leagues are sponsored by the Amsterdam Billiard Club (tel: 212-496-8180) and bowling leagues are ubiquitous at lanes throughout the city. American Youth Hostels (tel: 212-932-2300) organizes group bicycle trips.
- Other YMCAs, private health clubs, golf, tennis, squash and swimming clubs, and Park Department facilities are listed in the White and Yellow Pages. The median annual health club

190

fee is between $700 to $900, but virtually every sports facility, both indoor and outdoor, is available for a pittance through the Park Department.

Reminders and Suggestions

In prime-time basketball hours, many of New York's 1,000 outdoor and indoor basketball courts, operated by the Department of Parks and Recreation, are occupied by competitive and skilled players. To get into one of these games you've got to wait your turn and then prove you can play competitively.

Baseball and softball leagues are often made up of teams put together at workplaces, but at many of the city's hundreds of baseball diamonds, improvised teams may need an extra man or woman. The same goes for touch football, an Autumn sport.

This section has emphasized team sports in which the newcomer can become socially involved. But other sports like handball (a traditional New York pastime), tennis, swimming, horseback riding, golf (with public and private courses in the outer boroughs and suburbs), ice and roller skating, racquetball, and sailing are all available. More exotic sports (for New Yorkers), such as rugby, sea kayaking, and windsufing also have their devotees.

VOLUNTEERING

Doing volunteer work is an ideal way to accomplish an important goal and at the same time become integrated with New Yorkers and life in the city.

- The best source for volunteer opportunities is Richard Mintzer's *Volunteering in New York City: Your Guide to Working Small Miracles in the Big Apple*. The 15,000 volunteer opportunities include art and culture, zoos and parks, child care and tutorial, English teaching, family services, after-school programs, services for the homeless, libraries, senior services, and health and human services.

191

- **New York Cares** (tel: 212-228-5000) is a volunteer referral service that can help you find your niche within these or other areas of interest. Try the New York Cares website at: *http://www.ny.cares.org/*
- The **Mayor's Voluntary Action Center** (tel: 212-788-7550) is another ideal source of information on volunteer opportunities

WHEN NO ONE ELSE CAN HELP . . .

One universal strategy for getting things done when all other strategies fail is to approach an activist or advocacy group involved in community issues. These may include housing activists, legal defense organizations, and Hispanic, African-American, women's, and gay and lesbian groups. A whole pamphlet would be required to list all of New York's issue- or ethnic-oriented advocacy groups. A bookstore with pamphlets from many of these activist groups is **Pathfinder Books** (call 212-741-0690 for the location nearest you). The **Women's Center for Education and Career Advancement** (tel: 212-964-8934) and **Lambda Legal Defense and Education Fund**, a civil rights organization for lesbians, gay men, and people with HIV/AIDS (tel: 212-809-8585) are examples of such organizations. **WBAI-FM** (99.5 MHz on the dial) is a listener-sponsored radio station that can give you leads about community issues. Another ideal location to pick up pamphlets on advocacy groups is the **Unitarian Church** (tel: 212-639-9385), 1157 Lexington Avenue at 80th Street . The **Cathedral of St. John the Divine** (1045 Amsterdam Avenue at 112th Street), and last but not least, the **Riverside Church** (490 Riverside Drive at 122nd Street), are also involved in activist issues. Some of the city's great activists have been connected with the Riverside Church.

FURTHER READING

Books listed in this section are readily available in bookstores and libraries throughout North America. Readers abroad can obtain most of these books through Amazon.com (website at *http://www.amazon.com*).

To get the best feeling for the city's historical sense of place, I'd recommend four books and a film. Robert Caro's biography of Robert Moses, titled *The Power Broker: Robert Moses and the Fall of New York* (1974), covers significant changes in the structure and personality of this city during the twentieth century. Three other books, published more recently, will help readers understand today's New York: *All the Nations Under Heaven: An Ethnic and Racial History of New York City* by Frederick Bender and David Reimers (a contemporary history of immigrant New Yorkers); Janet Abu-Lughod's anthology *From Urban Village to East Village: The Battle for New York's Lower East Side* (a detailed account explaining the dynamics of neighborhood change in New York); and finally, Tom Wolfe's *The Bonfire of the Vanities* (not just an exciting novel, but also a compendium of realistic Manhattan prototypes—including several characters based on historical personalities). An ideal companion to Wolfe's novel is the film *A Bronx Tale*, starring Robert DeNiro, which will help newcomers get the feel for New York's deepest and darkest realities.

A grasp of the local history is vital for a newcomer's orientation. More obviously, pragmatic books deal with the nuts and bolts of adjusting to the city. Clara Hemphill's *The Parents' Guide to New York City's Best Public Elementary Schools* was published in 1997, but given its success, you should find an updated version by now. One of the few guidebooks that shuns the usual tourist schlock is

Richard Laermer's *Native's Guide to New York: Advice with attitude for people who live here-and visitors we like*, which is regularly updated. Christopher Sulavick's *NYC for Free* is useful for entertainment and service alternatives. More crucial may be John Castle and John Connolly's *How to Find the Best Doctors*. To help avoid medical problems, New York is an ideal place to remain fit. The *New York Running Guide: the 44 best routes in the NYC area* and the *New York Walk Book* are both recent publications with practical information in an attractive format. For active job hunters, *The Metropolitan New York Job Bank: the Job Hunter's Guide to Metro New York* contains 7,700 employer profiles, and 90 on-line career resources.

Books that perceptively delve into New York's cultural subtleties include *New Yawk Tawk: a Dictionary of New York City Expressions*, which is more than a linguistic treasure, since many local expressions serve to illustrate cultural idiosyncrasies. Have special fun with the letter "r," which disappears (*dissapeahs*) in words like *New Yawk*, *mothah* (mother), and *I feel bettah* (better), only to reappear where it shouldn't be after words ending in *a*: *Marther* instead of Martha, and *drahmer* instead of drama. And then there's Brooklynese, which has it's own tang. Daniel Drennan's *The New York Diaries*, a humorous diary of city life, includes chapters on stress and the subway culture. Avery Corman's *The Old Neighborhood* is a novel that rings authentic, dealing with the urban-suburban dichotomy and New York's basketball culture. Woody Allen's film *Mighty Aphrodite* is a take on New York's class differences from a fumbling Upper East Side perspective.

The recent classic, urbanologist Ray Oldenburg's *The Great Good Place*, makes various references to New York as compared to other cities in the world, and provides an engagingly written sociological foundation for identifying urban quality of life, as does the journal *Urban Quality Indicators* (for subscription information, write: Suite 239, 1756 Plymouth Road, Ann Arbor, MI 48105 or call 313-996-8610).

THE AUTHOR

Mark Cramer triangulates his life between Paris, France, La Paz, Bolivia, and New York (thus obligating his son Marcus to learn three languages by the age of 10). His favorite cities in the world are Paris, New York, Havana, Barcelona, and San Francisco — not necessarily in that order.

Cramer has written books on Bolivia, California, Mexico, and Cuba for Times Editions' *Culture Shock!* series. His *Funky Towns USA: The Best Alternative, Eclectic, and Visionary Places* (1995) was featured on CNN, written up in more than 50 newspapers and journals, and is used as a text at several universities.

During the day, you can find Cramer at the race track. At night, look for him at any club where you can find music in the style of Thelonius Monk or Cuban *son*. If you see someone on the New York subway or Paris metro reading Charles Bukowski, it's probably him.

INDEX

Praise for other books written by Mark Cramer:

Culture Shock! Bolivia

"Many South American travel guides are simply exhaustive tomes of statistics, histories and tips, failed attempts to intimately cover all the bases. These books are for the stereotypical traveler who wants to skirt all the main tourist stops and go home . . . Maybe they should take a few tips from Mark Cramer, author of *Culture Shock! Bolivia*. The book culls the most provocative, juiciest aspects of the country . . . Cramer has been able to submerge himself deep into Bolivian culture and current events, to discover the country's disparate attractions and reveal the catalytic events that have shaped today's Bolivia."

— Erik Loza, *Bolivian Times*

"*Culture Shock! Bolivia* is not only useful for foreign travelers but also for Bolivian tourists who have grown up knowing only fragments of the land where we were born."

— Pablo Solón, *Bolivian historian*

Culture Shock! Cuba

"I really thought *Culture Shock! Cuba* was informative and helpful. I will have my students buy it for their trip to Cuba."

— Jon Torgerson,
Department of Philosophy and Religion, Drake University

Culture Shock! Mexico

"*Culture Shock! Mexico* can be a great help for any foreigners who visit our country, to help them better enjoy, better understand, and better fit into our complex nation."

— Dr. José María Muriá,
President of the Institute of Graduate Studies, Colegio de Jalisco